RULES AND PROCEDURE OF
QUASI-JUDICIAL FUNCTION

DOMESTIC ENQUIRY

RULES AND PROCEDURE OF QUASI-JUDICIAL FUNCTION
DOMESTIC ENQUIRY

Vivek Krishna

ZORBA BOOKS

ZORBA BOOKS

Published in India by Zorba Books, 2017

Website: www.zorbabooks.com
Email: info@zorbabooks.com

Copyright © Vivek Krishna

ISBN Print Book - 978-93-86407-62-7

Zorba Books Pvt. Ltd.(opc)
Gurgaon, INDIA

Printed at Repro Knowledgecast Limited, Thane

Dedicated to

My Spiritual Guru
Swami Sadafal Dev ji Maharaj

PREFACE TO THE EDITION

Discipline is of paramount importance in any organization. Indiscipline leads to Industrial Relations problem. It affects the morale of the employees. Industrial Relations problem has made some of the leading companies to become a thing of the past. It is true for companies both in private sector and public Sector, under the control of the government. In the recent past some of the most reputed Companies have witnessed the worst scenes of industrial relations, resulting in blood- shed and casualty. The tact of handling the problems relating to indiscipline keeps an executive on a high pedestal in any organization. The knowledge of conducting domestic or departmental enquiry forms an inseparable part of skill set that is required to tackle the problems of indiscipline and industrial relations. Lack of skill inside an organization is forcing the employers to engage Labour Consultants and Advocates to conduct domestic or departmental enquiries in cases of indiscipline.

Domestic or departmental enquiry is a quasi-judicial function. The concept of domestic enquiry as a quasi-judicial function has been discussed in the opening chapter of this book. The enquiries are conducted following the Rules of Natural Justice. A full chapter (Chapter II) has been dedicated to the Rules of Natural Justice for a comprehensive understanding of the subject. Many a times, the various terms relating to domestic enquiry are used without accurate and proper understanding of the same. This problem has been dealt in Chapter III in this book where important and common terms used in domestic enquiry have been crisply, but completely, described. The roles of three important functionaries in domestic enquiry cases, the enquiry officer, the presenting officer and the disciplinary authority, have been mentioned in a separate chapter(Chapter IV) for a quick reference, and clear understanding of the roles and responsibilities of these three important functionaries. The provisions of the Evidence Act, strictly speaking, are not applicable in cases of domestic enquiry. However, a broad understanding of the various types of the evidences and witnesses, and their importance in deciding a case, is required for absolute understanding of the subject of domestic enquiry. A complete chapter (Chapter V) has been dedicated to cater to this need of the readers. The chief part i.e., the procedure of domestic enquiry has been mentioned in a short and substantial manner in Chapter VI. The interventions by the Court in erroneous and deliberate cases of dismissal, discharge or demotion (reduction in rank) orders passed by the employers is an important topic without which the understanding of the subject of domestic enquiry would be incomplete. A wrongfully dismissed, discharged or demoted employee gets relief from the Court. The subject has been dealt in Chapter VII. Some of the provisions of the Acts or Statutes have direct bearing on the subject domestic enquiry. This has been mentioned selectively in Chapter VIII.

Case citations, which are *Stare Decisis (legal principle of determining points in litigation according to precedent)* have been mentioned very selectively.

All care has been taken to fend off mistakes and errors. I apologize ,however, for any inadvertent mistake or error, and the same should be ignored.

I express my deep sense of gratitude to all who have contributed directly or indirectly in completing this book.

I very sincerely believe that the book will be of good use to the readers.

2016   **VIVEK KRISHNA**

CONTENTS

CHAPTER I

DOMESTICS ENQUIRY:
A QUASI-JUDICIAL FUNCTION

INTRODUCTION

An orderliness in system, and maintenance of discipline, is required in every organization whether government, or public sector or any private establishment. Orderliness and discipline requires that established rules and regulations of the organization must be properly observed by the employees of the organization. An employee who violates the established rules and regulations of the organization must be appropriately punished so that he does not repeat such act. The act of punishment works as a deterrent, both for him and for other employees in the organization. On the other hand, some restraints are required on the powers of an employer to punish the employees working under him. An arbitrary and capricious act of punishment by the employer may defeat the very purpose of punishment. It is, therefore, necessary to establish a fair and honest procedure in the organization to enquire into the alleged act of misconduct by an employee so that an appropriate punishment may be awarded to him. This procedure in common parlance is called 'domestic enquiry' procedure. It is termed as domestic enquiry because the enquiry is conducted 'in-house' by the persons employed in the organization. Of late, legal practitioners are engaged by some employers to conduct domestic enquiry. However, still largely the domestic or departmental enquiries are conducted by none other than the persons employed in the organization.

The function of domestic enquiry is a quasi-judicial function. The term 'quasi' means 'almost', 'nearly' or 'resembling', and the term 'judicial' means 'of or pertaining to administering of justice' (Funk and Wagnall's, Standard Desk Dictionary). Since justice is dispensed in domestic enquiry, it is considered a 'judicial' procedure. But, because it does not contain all the features of a judicial process, it is regarded as a 'Quai-judicial' procedure. It only resembles a legal or judicial procedure. Like a judicial procedure, in domestic enquiry the enquiry officer acts like a judge and decides a disputing matter of alleged misconduct between the two disputing parties, the management and the charged employee, on the basis of evidences and witnesses produced at the enquiry by the two parties of the case. In domestic enquiry all the requirements of a law court are not required to be observed because it is not a completely legal procedure. The purpose of enquiry is only to find out the veracity of charges levelled against an employee. The strict rules of Evidence Act and procedures of court, in case of summoning witnesses, are not required to be observed in a domestic enquiry. Still, the basic rules that must be observed in deciding a judicial matter are necessarily observed. These rules are called the rules of natural justice. Since the procedures of domestic enquiry are not based upon any legal procedure backed by any statute, the observance of natural justice acquires phenomenal importance in deciding a case.

Enquiries by management into the misconduct of workmen are of a quasi-judicial nature and it is of utmost importance that such enquiry should be conducted in manner so as to inspire confidence in the impartiality of the enquiring officer. *Western India Match Company v. Paratha Sarathi (1956) I LLJ 151.*

The rules of natural justice are basic common sense propositions to judiciously and fairly dispense justice in any disputing matter. An enquiry officer in a domestic enquiry is required to act in good faith, hear both the sides, provide full opportunity to the parties to adequately present their case, and to correct and controvert any relevant statement prejudicial to them. *Bhikam Bobla v. Punjab State AIR 1963 Punj. 255.*

PREREQISITES OF A QUASI-JUDICIAL FUNCTION

It has been mentioned earlier that domestic enquiry is a quasi-judicial function. It may be of some significance here to mention the pre-requisites of a quasi-judicial function. The pre-requisites of a quasi judicial function are as follows:

1. The body exercising the quasi-judicial function must have some legal authority

It is important to know that from where the quasi-judicial function of domestic enquiry gets legal authority. We will examine this for the employees working in (a) government, (b) semi-government or public sector and (c) private sector organizations.

(a) Employees working in government organizations

The employees in government organizations or government departments, Central or State, get protection in service by the Constitution of India under Article 311 of the Constitution. The said Article of the Constitution reads as below mentioned:

Article 311. Dismissal, removal or reduction in rank of persons employed in civil capacities under the Union or a State.

(1) No person who is a member of a civil service of the Union or an all India service or a civil service of a State or holds a civil post under the Union or a State shall be dismissed or removed by a authority subordinate to that by which he was appointed.

(2) No such person as aforesaid shall be dismissed or removed or reduced in rank except after an inquiry in which he has been informed of the charges against him and given a reasonable opportunity of being heard in respect of those charges; Provided that where it is proposed after such inquiry, to impose upon him any such penalty, such penalty may be imposed on the basis of the evidence adduced during such inquiry and it shall not be necessary to give such person any opportunity of making representation on the penalty proposed; Provided further that this clause shall not apply-

    (a) where a person is dismissed or removed or reduced in rank on the ground of conduct which has led to his conviction on a criminal charge; or

    (b) where the authority empowered to dismiss or remove a person or to reduce him in rank is satisfied that for some reason, to be recorded by that authority in writing, it is not reasonably practicable to hold such inquiry; or

    (c) where the President or the Governor, as the case may be, is satisfied that in the interest of the security of the State, it is not expedient to hold such inquiry.

(3) If, in respect of any such person as aforesaid, a question arises whether it is reasonably practicable to hold such inquiry as is referred to in clause (2), the decision thereon of the authority empowered to dismiss or remove such person or to reduce him in rank shall be final.

It is clearly mentioned in 311 (2) that if any person who is employed in government service, Central or State, he cannot be dismissed, or removed from service nor can he be reduced in rank without holding an enquiry, and he will be clearly informed of the charges mentioned against him. He must also get an opportunity of being heard in respect of those charges. This provision of the Constitution of India provides legal authority to the quasi-judicial function of domestic enquiry for the employees employed in service of the government.

However, the same article 311 (2) states that an enquiry may not be necessary in certain cases where it is not reasonable to hold such enquiry or where it may not expedient owing to security of the State. However, such a decision of not holding an enquiry should not be arbitrary and reasons for not holding the enquiry must be stated in writing.

(b) Employees working in public sector or semi-government organizations

The public sector organizations or semi-government organizations or Corporations formed under an Act of the Parliament make rules and regulations of service for the employees working under them. The rules and regulations of service framed for the employees contains such provisions which define the acts of misconduct and procedure to take disciplinary action against an employee. The rules and regulations thus framed make it obligatory for the employers in public sector organizations to conduct an enquiry into the alleged act of misconduct against any employee before awarding any punishment. State Bank of India (Supervisory Staff) Services Rules, PNB Officer's Employees (D&A) Regulation etc. are examples of such rules and regulations. The Industrial Employment (Standing Orders) Act,1946 is also applicable for public sector industrial undertakings.

(c) Employees working in private Sector organizations

The Industrial Employment (Standing Orders) Act, 1946 is applicable in case of employees working in Private sector organizations. The Standing Orders Act requires the industrial establishments working in private sector to frame and get certified standing orders to regulate the conditions of service of workmen employed in them. The Standing Orders of an organization, thereby, gets statutory base. Once framed and certified, the Standing Orders becomes binding on the employers and the employee. The Standing Orders of a Company essentially contains provisions regarding suspension or dismissal for misconduct, and acts of omissions which constitute misconduct. This requires following the procedure of domestic enquiry.

It is abundantly clear that it is essential to hold domestic or departmental enquiry before awarding punishment to an employee. Such enquiries have got legal sanctity. This is true for employees in government, semi-government or public sector and private sector undertakings.

2. The body exercising the quasi-judicial function must perform some judicial nature of work .

It is essential for a quasi-judicial authority to perform judicial nature of work. This is true for domestic enquiry where the enquiry officer acts like a judge and performs judicial activity. The management and the charged employee present their evidences and witnesses in the enquiry. The enquiry officer provides opportunity to the delinquent employee to cross examine the witnesses and evidences of the prosecution side. He provides equal opportunity to the management representative to cross examine the witnesses and evidences provided by the defence side. On the basis of the records produced at the enquiry, the enquiry officer writes his findings and determines whether the allegation against the delinquent employee is proved or not. Almost, similar procedure is adopted in a court of law. Thus, the enquiry officer performs like a judicial authority as his act involves work of some judicial nature.

3. The body exercising the quasi-judicial function must settle a point of dispute, between two disputing parties.

The enquiry officer settles a point of dispute in a domestic enquiry. The point of dispute revolves round the allegation of misconduct on the charge-sheeted employee which the prosecution side or the management representative tries to prove, and the charge-sheeted employee or the defence side tries to disprove. The dispute is settled on the basis of evidences and witnesses presented at the enquiry. The enquiry officer reaches at a logical finding based on the records.

It may be mentioned, however, that the enquiry officer only gives his point of view in relation to the charges levelled on the employee on the basis of the records available before him. It is his individual judgment based on facts presented at the enquiry.

4. A quasi- judicial function allows reviews, revisions and appeals.

A judicial decision is open to reviews, revisions and appeals. This is true for domestic enquiry. First of all, the outcome of the domestic enquiry is the finding of the enquiry officer. This is the individual judgment of the enquiry officer based on evidences on record. The punishing authority may or may not agree with the views and findings of the enquiry officer. Secondly, in domestic enquiry before awarding punishment of discharge and dismissal the provision of a second opportunity or second show-cause may exist where the punishing authority may review his expressed decision of inflicting a punishment of discharge or dismissal. This is based on the logical reasoning provided by the delinquent employee against such proposed punishment. Thirdly, the decision of an employer is subject to review and revision by the Law Courts where the punishment of dismissal or discharge awarded by an employer is challenged in a court of law by the aggrieved employee. The Law Courts can provide relief to an aggrieved employee by setting aside an arbitrary dismissal or discharge order passed by the employer.

5. A quasi-judicial decision does not create new law.

A judicial decision sets precedent. In the areas where specific statutory provisions are not mentioned, a judicial decision creates a new law. This is not true in case of a quasi-judicial decision. A quasi-judicial decision does not set a precedent. It does not create a new law. This is a very major difference between a quasi-judicial act and a judicial act. The decision in case of a domestic enquiry is peculiar to that case only. It is not necessarily followed in exact manner in other similar type of cases. A domestic enquiry decision, obviously, does not create a new law.

6. A quasi-judicial body need not follow strict judicial rules of evidence and procedure.

A quasi-judicial body need not follow strict judicial rules of evidence and procedure. The Evidence Act is not followed in strict sense in a case of domestic enquiry. In domestic enquiry an enquiry officer cannot summon witness like the judge of a court of law. The enquiry officer cannot force the attendance of a witness. Moreover, an enquiry officer in a domestic enquiry only verifies the allegations levelled against a charge-sheeted employee. Like the Judge of a court of law he is not authorize to pronounce punishment if the charge is established against the delinquent employee on the basis of evidences adduced at the enquiry.

The provisions of Evidence Act is not strictly followed in domestic enquiry. In criminal prosecution if there is any doubt then benefit of doubt goes to the accused. It is not the test in departmental enquiry. The evidence may be sufficient for departmental enquiry but not for criminal case. *Chulsa Tea Co. v. Workmen Cal Gaz.,Part I-C,dt. 31.07.1969, p.285 (IT).*

In the absence of rules governing its procedure the domestic tribunal is not bound by the ordinary rules of evidence and it is not bound to follow the procedure of the code of law. *Trustees of Port of Bombay v. Bombay Port Trust Employees' Union 1956 ICR 552 (LAT).*

7. A quasi-judicial function rests on theories of natural justice.

The proceedings in civil cases are governed by Code of Civil Procedure, and the proceedings in criminal cases are governed by Code of Criminal Procedure. In case of a quasi-judicial function there is no statute to govern the proceedings. Therefore, the quasi-judicial function rests heavily on theories of natural justice.

The theories of natural justice follow rules which ensure fair play and reasonableness. It prevents miscarriage of justice by following very fundamental rules of dispensing justice.

The importance of natural justice has been outlined by Allahabad High Court in case of *Mukhtar Singh v. State of U.P.* when it was mentioned regarding the principles of natural justice that the principles of natural justice are those rules which have been laid down by the Courts as being the minimum protection of the rights of the individual against the arbitrary procedure that may be adopted by a judicial or quasi-judicial authority while making an order affecting those rights. These rules are intended to prevent such authority from doing injustice. *Mukhtar Singh v. State of U.P. AIR 1957, All 297, 301.*

Thus, it is clear that a procedure of conducting enquiry into the charges of misconduct of an employee is required to be firmly established in any organization for the purpose of awarding punishment in a fair and impartial manner. This is not a choice before the employer. The provisions contained in the Constitution and Statute like, the Industrial Employment (Standing Orders) Act, 1946 and The Public Servants (Inquiries) Act, 1850 also make it mandatory. The quasi-judicial function of domestic enquiry follows the rules of natural justice which will be discussed in detail in the next chapter.

CHAPTER II

THEORIES OF NATURAL JUSTICE (JUS NATURALE)

The main plank on which the quasi-judicial act of domestic or departmental enquiry rests is the theory of natural justice. It is of importance to note that proceedings before the civil court are governed by the Code of Civil Procedure; criminal proceedings are governed by the Criminal Procedure Code, but in respect of departmental enquiries, no detailed guidelines have been codified. In the absence of any codified law, proceedings under departmental enquiries are mainly governed by the principles of natural justice.

The term 'natural justice' is derived from the Roman words 'Jus Naturale', which means principles of natural law, justice, equity, and good conscience. These principles did not originate from any divine power, but are the outcome of the necessity of judicial thinking, as well as the necessity to evolve the norms of fair play. These are the principles which every disciplinary authority should follow while taking any decision, which may adversely affect the rights of individuals. It is to be seen that rules of natural justice are not codified anywhere; they are procedural in nature and their aim is to ensure delivery of justice to the parties. These rules are intended to prevent such authority from doing injustice.

Rules of natural justice are not rules embodied in any statute. The concept of natural justice has evolved with the evolution of society, as well as legal jurisprudence. These rules are being observed in India, and other parts of the world since time immemorial. These rules have become a part and parcel of the law, as well as procedure. These may be implied from the nature of the duty to be performed under a statute. What particular rule of natural justice should be applied depends on the facts and circumstances of each case.

The rules of natural justice are applied not only in judicial decisions, but also in administrative decisions. With the passage of time, the old distinction between a judicial act and an administrative act has withered away. Orders of the disciplinary authority, which involve civil consequence, must be consistent with the rules of natural justice, otherwise the orders are likely to be set aside by the law courts.

The basic principle of natural justice applicable in case of any judicial nature of work or administrative decision is that the authority taking a decision should not carry any bias towards one side or the other. The doctrine of bias means that no man shall be a judge in ones own case and justice should not only be done but should manifestly and undoubtedly seem to be done.

If an enquiry officer conducting a quasi-judicial function is bias, or is in such a position that a bias may exist in his decision then he should not take part in that enquiry. An enquiry conducted by a biased enquiry officer is considered invalid.

G. Nageswar Rao v. A.P.S.R.T. Corporation, AIR 1959 SC 308.

It is a set principle that one who is interested in the litigation is already biased against the party concerned. *Mukhtar Singh v. State AIR 1957 All HC 297 (30)*

THEORIES OF NATURAL JUSTICE ARE SUBSERVIENT TO STATUTORY PROVISIONS

The principles of natural justice are subservient to statutory provisions. They are not the rule of law that can override the codified laws of the land. In the case of *A.K. Kraipak V. Union of India (AIR 1970 SC 150), the Supreme Court said that the aim of natural justice is to secure justice or to put it negatively to prevent miscarriage of justice. These rules can operate only in areas not covered by any law validly made, in other words, they do not supplant law, but supplement it.*

The legislature can prescribe whether the theory of natural justice will be followed in a particular case, and in such a situation the law court respects the direction of the legislature. *Ramjibhai Ukabhai Parmer v. Manilal Purushottam Solanki AIR 1960 Guj 19.*

THEORIES OF NATURAL JUSTICE ARE NOT LIKE FUNDAMENTAL RIGHTS

As already stated earlier the theories of natural justice are subservient to statutory provisions. The theories of natural justice that govern the quasi-judicial functions do not find a mention in the Constitution of India. The "Due Process" theory which governs the acts of quasi-judicial functions in America finds a place in the American Constitution. But, the theories of natural justice which are similar to "Due process" (Justified, Reasonable and Proper Process) law of America do not find a place in the Constitution of India. They are not as sacred in law as the fundamental rights of the citizen positively mentioned in Part- III of the Constitution of India.

Still, the neglect of theories of natural justice is considered bad in law specially where no specific statute passed by the Parliament is available to govern the act of any quasi judicial body. It is important, therefore, to understand with clarity the various theories of natural justice.

The various theories of natural justice and their implications in departmental enquiries have been mentioned below. For the purpose of understanding the theories have been divided into four categories -

   I.   Relating to Rights of a Delinquent
   II.   Relating to Prosecutor
   III.   Relating to Judges and Judgement
   IV.   Relating to Punishment

I.RELATING TO RIGHTS OF A DELINQUENT

1. "No one can be prohibited from making use of several defences".

(Nemo prohibetur plures negotiationes sive artes exercere)

No one is restrained from exercising several kinds of business or arts. In judicial and quasi-judicial context or in the rule of natural justice it means that a person must get all reasonable opportunities to defend himself. There should not be any restriction on his right to take several defences available to him. For making use of several defences it is required first that the delinquent must have a clear understanding that what allegations have been levelled against him. Then only he can prepare his defences. In the case of domestic enquiry, a delinquent employee must get a formal, specific and written charge-sheet that clearly contains the charges levelled against him. The first defence for the delinquent employee is to provide an explanation to the charge-sheet wherein he can mention his innocence assigning reasons thereof.

The second opportunity for defence for a delinquent employee arises when the management refuses to accept the explanation to the charge-sheet, and proceeds with a full fledged enquiry into the charges. In the enquiry the charged employee has the right to cross examine all the witnesses and evidences that purport to prove him guilty. The employee gets the right to present his witnesses and facts on record, of course, subject to cross examination by the presenting officer of the management. If the charged employee is prevented in any way in exercising these rights then the enquiry gets grossly vitiated and is liable to be set aside by the Court.

The third opportunity of defence is available to the charged employee when his explanation is sought before awarding a harsh punishment of discharge or dismissal which he can counter on the ground that such punishment would be out of proportion for the offence or misconduct committed by him. This depends on the merits of the case and specific rules and regulations relating to provision for seeking such explanation from the delinquent employee before awarding punishment, as aforesaid.

If the charged employee feels that at any stage during the enquiry the action of the enquiry officer is biased against him or that the punishment awarded to him by the management goes out of proportion then he can move the Law court to seek justice for himself.

A charged employee must exhaust all courses of action available to him in his defence. If he is prohibited from the same then it amounts to unjustice.

2 "No one ought to be a witness in his own cause".
(Nemo debet esse testis in sua propria causa)

The principle of natural justice says that no one ought to be a witness in ones own case. An employee should not be compelled to give any witness against himself in his own case. A fair judgement cannot be given on the basis of that incriminating statement. A statement taken by force or by other illegitimate method that incriminates a person is liable to be discarded. If a judgement is pronounced on the basis of that incriminating statement then it will be a violation of natural justice.

II. RELATING TO PROSECUTOR:

3. "The burden of proof lies on the plaintiff or the complainant".
(Actore incumbit onus probandi) Or, "The necessity of proving the charge lies on him who brings the charge" *(Probandi necessitas incumbit ei qui agit)*

The rule of natural justice says that the burden of proof lies on the plaintiff or the complainant who brings the charge.

In departmental enquiry the management alleges misconduct on any employee, therefore, it is management's duty to prove that such omission or commission which constitutes misconduct has been committed by the employee. If the management fails to prove the charge then the employee is considered to be innocent. However, such occasions are rare because the management issues charge-sheet to an employee only when there is sufficient evidence against that employee.

The general rule of law is that a person is considered to be innocent till the charges levelled against him are undisputedly proved. It is because by merely making allegations a person does not become guilty of the charges. It is the onerous duty of the plaintiff or the complainant to prove the charge. If the charges are not proved, and the allegations come out to be false, then the employee on whom the charges are levelled may even counter allege of being victimized or wrongly framed by ulterior motives of the management.

III. RELATING TO JUDGES AND JUDGEMENT:

4. "No one ought to be a judge in his own cause".

(Nemo debet esse judex in propria causa)

The principle of natural justice requires that no person can be a judge in his own cause. *Sunil Kumar Ghose v. Ajit Kumar, AIR 1969 Cal 492.*

In departmental proceedings, if the enquiry is conducted by a person who is himself a party to the dispute then the report of enquiry will not hold good. It is liable to be set aside. If that person becomes the judge who is a party to the dispute then possibility is that justice will not be pronounced without bias. The element of bias will vitiate the case.

One who has interest in the case will be considered biased against the party concerned. *Mukhtar Singh v. State, AIR 1957 All 297 (30).*

In the industrial dispute cases, the question of bonafides or mala fides of the employer carries importance. If it is shown that an employer was actuated by a desire to victimise a workman, that may in some cases introduce an infirmity in the order of the disciplinary authority. This is another reason why the enquiry in industrial matters should be held with scrupulous regard to the rules of natural justice.

It should be noted that the enquiry officer cannot be the person who is himself a complainant or is related to any of the witnesses or the concerned employee, or has ill-will or malice against any of the person concerned.

It has been rightly said, therefore, that justice should not only be done but manifestly and undoubtedly be seem to be done. When a person is himself a party to the dispute then conduct of enquiry by that person is likely to raise suspicion.

5. "No one can be at once suitor and judge".

(Nemo potest esse simul actor et judex)

The principle of natural justice requires that no one can be at once suitor and judge. In departmental enquiry this principle is applicable in two situations-

- It bars conduct of enquiry by that person who is himself a party to the dispute.
- It bars the person who is conducting the enquiry to assume the role of management representative or presenting officer at any time during the process of the enquiry.

There is possibility of a bias if the suitor, who has made the allegation, himself becomes the judge and conducts the enquiry. It will be practically not possible for the person who has to prove the allegation would remain an unbiased judge. On a number of occasion the Law courts have declared the enquiry as invalid and set aside the enquiry report where the enquiry officer himself assumed the role of management representative and assisted in proving the charge against the delinquent employee.

6. "No judge should import his private knowledge of the facts into a Case".

(Non refert quid notum sit judici, si noium non sit in forma judicit)

A judge should base his judgement only on the basis of the facts placed before him during the proceedings of the case. Alternatively, it is also said that what is known to the judge does not matter. A judge, or an enquiry officer, must confine his knowledge to the facts brought out in the enquiry.

The enquiry officer should not import his personal knowledge in writing the enquiry report and findings because it can create a bias.

The charged employee may not be aware, in all possibility, with the knowledge of the enquiry officer which he uses in writing the report or determining the case. Therefore, he misses the opportunity of cross examining that fact. Moreover, the personal knowledge which the enquiry officer imports in deciding a case may not be true in relation to that case.

The case of C. P. Govil v. Union of India presents a good example in this regard. The enquiry officer based his report on the basis of information collected from the personal file of the employee. Since this information was not brought in the enquiry before the employee it was considered violation of the established norms. *C. P. Govil v. Union of India 1965 DLT 16 (DB).*

A judge or an enquiry officer must rely on the evidences brought at the enquiry, and confine to that only. A careful and proper scrutiny of the records itself gives sufficient reasons to decide the case one way or the other.

7. **"It is duty of the judge to determine according to what is alleged and Proved".** *(Judicis est judicare secundum allegata et probate)Or,* **"The court has nothing to do with what is not brought before it".** *(Nihil habet forum ex scena)*

In departmental enquiry the enquiry officer should rely on facts and evidences brought at the enquiry. The enquiry report should be based on material evidence produced at the enquiry. Every finding of the enquiry officer must be rooted in facts deposed at the enquiry.

When it is said the court has nothing to do with what is not brought before it then it simply means that the findings of the judge or the enquiry officer should not be based on extraneous considerations. It should completely depend on record what has been brought before the enquiry because in that case the alleged employee gets an opportunity to cross examine that record.

So far as the finding of the judge or the enquiry officer is concerned, nothing should come to the delinquent employee as a surprise. He must have had the opportunity to see and cross examine the records, statements or material evidences used to prove the allegation against him. It is the duty of the enquiry officer to determine *a case* only according to those materials which are on record.

In the case of *Anjali v. SBI*, termination from bank service was based on findings which were founded on pure suspicion, and surmises without subscribing, any reason. On appeal, it was held that the order was not a speaking order, with no application of mind to the points raised by the employee. Hence, termination from service was quashed, as the principles of natural justice were violated. Allegation and proof was not based on material facts which could be brought before the Enquiry Officers. *Anjali v. SBI 1993 (2) Bank CLR 372.*

Now it is being held by the Courts that the order passed by an enquiry officer or administrative agency must be a 'speaking order'. A speaking order carries the reasons behind the judgement. If the order is not supported by reasons, it will amount to violation of the rules of natural justice. If the order of the enquiry officer would be based on extraneous factors and not on what is alleged and proved at the enquiry then it would be difficult for him to pass a speaking verdict.

If the order is passed with reasons, only then will it show that there was proper appreciation of evidence by the disciplinary authority, otherwise the aggrieved party will not be in a position to demonstrate before the appellate authority, as to the manner in which the order passed by the initial authority is bad or suffers from a particular illegality.

It would be observed that about three or four decades ago, it was not required that the administrative order or the order of disciplinary authority must be supported with reasons. It was held by the Supreme Court in the case of *Som Dutt v. Union Of India (AIR 1969 SC 414)* that there is no rule of natural justice that a statutory tribunal should always and in every case give reason in support of the decision. But, with the evolution of natural justice, a new dimension of reasoned order has been added to these rules. There is a feeling among legal luminaries that the requirement of providing reasons for any decision gives an assurance that the evidence relating to the case has been duly considered by the authority.

The findings should also be supported by reasons because: it facilitates judicial review of findings of the enquiry officer; findings offer assurance to the parties that the decision is the outcome of rationality based on evidence as well as the records of the case; and it ensures against arbitrary or hasty action on the part of deciding authority.

8. "One who determines any matter without hearing both the sides, although he may have decided right, has not done justice". (*Qui aliquid statuerit, parte inaudita altera, acquum licet dexerit, haud acquum facerit) Or,* **"Hear the Other Side"** *(Audi Alterem Partem/* Audiatur et altera pars*).*

Departmental enquiries relating to the misconduct of individuals should conform to certain standards. One of the standards is that the person concerned must be given a fair and reasonable opportunity to defend himself. It means that no man should be condemned unheard and he has right to know the accusations levelled against him. He has also the right to know the premise on which such accusation is based, and a reasonable opportunity to adduce all relevant evidence in his defence.

'Hear the other side' besides being a requirement of the theory of natural justice is also a constitutional provision. The employees in civil nature of job under the government are protected by Article 311(2) of the Constitution of India when it states that "no person shall be dismissed or removed or reduced in rank except after an inquiry in which he has been informed of the charges against him and given a reasonable opportunity of being heard in respect of those charges".

'Hear the other side' cannot be stretched to any unreasonable extent. The consequences of not responding to this provision of natural justice is manifest in the case of *Nagar Palika, Nataur v. U.P. Public Services Tribunal, Lucknow, 1998 SCC (L&S)567*, when despite reminders, the employee neither submitted reply to the charge sheet, nor appeared before the enquiry officer, and neither did he inspect the records, in spite of the opportunity given to him then in such cases, the findings of the enquiry officer on the basis of the available records that the charges were proved, was held not violative of the rules of natural justice.

9. "Judge not too hastily".
(Ne seipsum praecipites in discriminem)

A judge should not be in a hurry to decide the case. A judge must not at once jump to a conclusion without considering completely and comprehensively all the facts and circumstances of the case, and without properly weighing all the evidences brought before him during the proceedings. When a judge or an enquiry officer rushes to a decision it gives an indication about his forming an opinion about the charged employee without properly weighing the evidences and records.

Since in departmental enquiry a charged employee does not get a benefit of doubt, it becomes all the more important for the enquiry officer to carefully weigh the evidences.

In criminal prosecution if there is any doubt then benefit of doubt goes to the accused. It is not the test in departmental enquiry. The evidence may be sufficient for departmental enquiry but not for criminal case. *Chulsa Tea Co. v. Workmen, Cal Gaz., Part I-C, dt. 31.07.1969, p.285.*

In the absence of rules governing its procedure the domestic tribunal is not bound by the ordinary rules of evidence and it is not bound to follow the procedure of the code of law. *Trustees of Port of Bombay v. Bombay Port Trust Employees' Union 1956 ICR 552 (LAT).*

It is said that justice should not only be done but it should be apparent that it has been properly done. That justice should not be done very hastily is a very reasonable proposition. But, the opposite of it is an equally valid proposition that justice delayed is justice denied. A judge should keep in mind both the propositions.

IV. RELATING TO PUNISHMENT :

10. "Let the punishment be proportionate to the offence".
(Culpa poena par esto)

The punishment must always be on the basis of the guilt of the person. Too harsh or too little a punishment is neglect of justice. The punishment awarded by an employee should not be too harsh as would create a demoralizing effect on the rest of the employees and would create several negative impacts including industrial relations problem, and at the same time punishment awarded should not be too little as would make a mockery of the whole system and would not act as a deterrent. There should be a balance. It is , therefore, the rule of natural justice maintains that punishment should be in proportion to the offence committed by the employee.

In case of departmental enquiry, and award of punishment by the employer to the employee, a review mechanism also lies with the Labour Court and Industrial Tribunal under Section 11 A of the Industrial Disputes Act. The Labour Court or Industrial Tribunal can interfere with the punishment awarded to an employee by the employer if the Court or tribunal maintains that the punishment awarded by the employer is out of proportion in relation to the offence committed by the employee and rule of natural justice in matter of awarding punishment has been violated. The Labour Court or Industrial Tribunal interferes in matters of punishment awarded to an employee in the best interest of the both the employee and the employer as well as in the larger interest of the industry and industrial relations.

The fact, however, cannot be denied that the rules of discipline in an industry lies in the hands of management. In the best interest of the smooth running of the industry no outside interference is allowed except when an employee is punished out of proportion in very indiscreet manner without having any regard to simple rule of natural justice.

11. "No one is punished twice for the same offence".
(Nemo bis punitur pro sodem delicto)

According to general rule no body should be punished twice for the same offence. Article 20 (2) of the Constitution of India affirms this principle and provides that no person shall be punished for the same offence more than once. This article of the constitution, however, has limited applicability in case of departmental enquiry.

An employer cannot punish an employee twice in succession, or in sequence, for the same offence. For example, an employer cannot first suspend an employee, and then after reconsidering the punishment dismiss the employee for the same offence committed by him. This will not be held valid.

An employer, however, can punish an employee and dismiss him from the service if the employee has been punished by the Law Courts under the Indian Penal Code for the same offence. Here, double punishment is inflicted upon the employee - one by the Law court under the Indian Penal Code and another by the employer under the rules of the organization or under the Standing Orders of the Company. The delinquent employee does not have a protection here under Article 20(2) of the Constitution.

The point to be kept in mind is that there are two authorities inflicting punishment here under two different procedures- one under the Code of Criminal Procedure and another under quasi-judicial procedure of domestic enquiry which extensively follows the rules of natural justice. The same authority is not inflicting double punishment.

It will still be considered violation of natural justice if the same authority inflicts punishment twice for the same offence which is not held good in the eyes of law.

Another important thing to consider here is that if two employees who have committed same or similar nature of offence then generally the punishment awarded to them by the management should be same. It should not be discriminatory that one employee has been awarded very hard punishment while the other employee has been awarded soft punishment. This discrimination also creates bad blood between the management and the employees.

Award of discriminatory punishment is considered violation of rule of natural justice. The two different types of punishment cannot weigh equal, and are not regarded in equal proportion. Hence, it is considered violation of natural justice. On some occasions, however, for the same offence habitual offenders are awarded higher punishment in comparison to those who commit the offence for the first time. This appears to be justified because such discrimination is backed by reason, and is not arbitrary. However, such discriminatory punishment depends on the nature of offence, and for serious nature of offence this discriminatory treatment is not allowed where even the first offender merits a harsh punishment of discharge or dismissal.

It would be seen that the rules of natural justice are flexible, and cannot be weighed in golden scales, nor can it be put in any straight-jacket. It depends on the extent to which the rights of an individual are affected. The role of these rules is to ensure justice to both the parties. Their contravention cannot be presumed, unless it can be shown that injustice has actually been done. In certain matters, only representation may be sufficient, while in others, full-fledged hearing and cross-examination may be necessary. What the courts have to examine is that whether non-observance of any of the rules is likely to prejudice any of the parties.

ALL THE RULES OF NATURAL JUSTICES MUST BE FOLLOWED :

All the rules of natural justice are important and should not be ignored by any quasi-judicial authority. If any rule of natural justice is violated in the disciplinary procedure then it is liable to vitiate the enquiry. The rules of natural justice apply from beginning to end when it comes to taking action against an employee for his alleged act of misconduct. The charges must be framed very specifically without any ulterior motive, proper communication of the charge-sheet to the delinquent employee should be ensured, an independent person should be appointed as enquiry officer to enquire into the charges levelled against the employee, all material facts, evidences and records on which the charge rests must be produced in the enquiry before the delinquent employee and he should get reasonable opportunity to cross-examine them, the delinquent employee must also get opportunity to present his case and witnesses from his side, findings of the enquiry must be based on records, and if the charge stands established the delinquent employee must be punished in proportion to the offence committed by him.

All the rules of natural justice must be understood properly for a clear understanding of the procedure of domestic or departmental enquiry. It is equally important to understand the definition and meaning of other important terms related to domestic or departmental enquiry. In the next chapter we will discuss the important terms related to domestic or departmental enquiry.

CHAPTER III

IMPORTANT TERMS RELATED TO DOMESTIC ENQUIRY

Domestic enquiry is a very important quasi-judicial bustle in the hands of employers to take action against an erring employee, and to maintain discipline in the organization. In fact, a lot of literature on the subject is available in pieces, here and there. But, it hardly helps in developing a concept of the subject. Our effort is to develop a deeper comprehension of the subject as well as the procedural simplicity with which a domestic enquiry should proceed. Wherever required case laws will be mentioned to illustrate a point under discussion.

It is important to mention here that very often a distinction is made between domestic enquiry in industrial enterprises and government or semi-government organizations. The fact, however, is that first, domestic or departmental enquiry is always a quasi-judicial function, and second, the theories of natural justice remain same, which are the guiding principles to conduct domestic enquiry. In substance, domestic enquiry remains same for industrial enterprises and government or semi-government organizations.

For a deeper understanding of the subject domestic enquiry it is imperative to understand first the different terms related with it. *The important terms used in domestic enquiry have been mentioned hereunder in alphabetic order.*

ADJOURNMENT OF ENQUIRY

Adjournment of enquiry means to defer or suspend the enquiry to a future date or time. When future date and time is not mentioned with the adjournment regarding resumption of the enquiry, it is called *indefinite adjournment (Sine die)*. When future date and time is mentioned with the adjournment regarding resumption of the enquiry it is called *temporary adjournment*.

Temporary adjournments cannot be avoided in domestic or departmental enquiry because of several reasons. It is not always possible to complete an enquiry continuously at a stretch. The requirement to prepare defence, production of important related documents and records, presentation of witnesses , cross examination of witnesses, etc. cannot be done in a mechanical manner. The complexity of the cases also adds in stretching the time. Meanwhile, the disputing parties and the witnesses may have other compelling reasons that prevent them from appearing at the enquiry as per schedule. All this necessitates adjournments of the enquiry.

The decisions of adjournment of the enquiry is solely the discretion of the enquiry officer. The adjournments of the enquiry form an integral part of the enquiry proceeding, and the adjournments with the reasons thereof, should be noted down by the enquiry officer in the proceedings of the enquiry.

It is duty, however, of all the parties connected with a case to complete the domestic enquiry without unreasonable delay. Any dilatory tactics to prolong the enquiry should be thwarted by the enquiry officer. It is not the right of charge-sheeted employee to ask for as many adjournments as he likes. *Tata Oil Mills Co. Ltd. v. Workmen, AIR 1965 SC 155.*

It may be noted that reasonable time must be allowed, both to the prosecution and defence side, for proper presentation of the case in the enquiry. Any reasonable request for adjournment of enquiry must be acceded to. *Denial of reasonable opportunity to present the case, or denial of any valid adjournment request may vitiate the enquiry.*

There cannot be any comprehensive list of grounds on which an enquiry may be adjourned by the enquiry officer without prejudice to any party, as it varies from situation to situation, but broadly some of the ground can be mentioned on which an enquiry officer normally grants adjournments. These are-

- To facilitate representation by a co-worker
- Absence of co-worker on any schedule date of enquiry due to authorized leave
- Absence of a witness due to valid reasons
- Illness of any concerned person when supported by a medical certificate
- Preparation of defence, like production of any document, record etc.
- Compelling personal reasons of any concerned person including the charge-sheeted employee, etc.

When the enquiry is adjourned, care should be taken to properly and formally inform the next date, time and place of enquiry to all concerned persons.

ARBITRARY ACTION

An act done capriciously made at pleasure without adequate determining principle, non rational and not done according to reason or judgement. (Black's Law Dictionary).

Any arbitrary decision of an authority, legally empowered to take such decision, is liable to be set aside by the Courts of law.

Article 14 of the Constitution discards any arbitrary action of the employer because it is considered violation of the fundamental rights. The Supreme court has decided in the case of *Hindustan Petroleum Corporation v. H. L. Trehan* , (1989) I SCC 764, that though the authority may have statutory power to take action without hearing it would be arbitrary to take action without hearing and thus violation of Article 14 of the Constitution.

BIAS

Bias is an inclination or leaning to present or hold a partial perspective. A biased person refuses to consider the possible merits of alternative points of view. Biased may mean one-sided, lacking a neutral viewpoint or not having an open mind. A bias can come in many forms and is also related to prejudice.

A person can become bias because of many reasons the principal ones being conflict of interest, favouritism, pecuniary interest, belief in infallibility of ones knowledge etc.

A biased person is not considered independent and fit to conduct an enquiry. If an element of bias is found in an enquiry, it is liable to be declared invalid and worthless.

When an enquiry officer or a judge conclusively believes that an employee is guilty and must be punished, then he is biased. A biased enquiry officer goes to any extent to prove the alleged employee guilty of the charges. The principle of natural justice requires that a biased person should not become a judge.

The principle of natural justice demands that the officer making enquiry should not be interested in bringing home the guilt to the accused at any cost. *A.R.S.Choudhary v. Union of India , AIR 1956 Cal 662.*

A mere apprehension of bias, though not founded on valid reasons, is capable of frustrating the process of enquiry. It is a matter of policy that justice should not merely be done but should appear to be done.

An unfavorable order, however, cannot be called a biased order. The burden of proving the bias lies on the delinquent employee. The delinquent employee has to show that any unfavourable order is a biased order. *Kapur Singh v. Union of India, AIR 1956 Punj. 58.*

BONA FIDE

Something done in good faith is called bona fide. The literal meaning of *'bona fide'* is 'genuine', 'true', 'legitimate'. The term 'bona fide' in disciplinary procedure means that at each step of disciplinary proceeding action is taken in honest and truthful manner. Otherwise, the action may get vitiated and become bad in the eyes of the law.

A *'bona fide'* action means that it has no ulterior or hidden motive, and is completely based on the merits of the case.

An order of the employer which is not *bona fide* and hints about the colourable exercise of power by the employer in punishing the employee is invariably invalidated by the Law Courts.

BURDEN OF PROOF

The term burden of proof simply means the onus or obligation to prove the fact. Burden of proof means leading the evidence first to prove the fact. The rule of natural justice says that the burden of proof lies on the plaintiff or the complainant *(Actore incombit onus probandi).*

In cases of departmental or domestic enquiry the burden of proof always lies with the management or the employer. Invariably, the management side or the prosecution side leads the evidence first.

CHARGE- SHEET

A charge –sheet is a formal document of accusation. In context of domestic or departmental enquiry, a charge- sheet contains in abstract the acts of omission or commission of a delinquent employee, which constitute misconduct according to the Standing Orders or set rules and regulations of the Company or the organization. If the allegation or charge levelled against a delinquent employee is established or confirmed in a fair and impartial enquiry, the employer is liable to punish the employee befitting the seriousness of the charge.

A charge-sheet is a show-cause notice which tells the delinquent employee that why a disciplinary action should not be initiated for the misconduct alleged to have been conducted by him. It leaves the scope for the employee to provide an explanation, and prove himself innocent in the enquiry held subsequently, if the explanation submitted by the employee is *prima facie* not very convincing to exonerate him from the charges.

An employee can be punished for his misconduct by his employer only on the basis of charge that is proved in a fair and impartial enquiry. If an employee is charged for certain misconduct, then the dismissal order cannot be justified on the ground that he is guilty of other misconducts. *Laxmi Devi Sugar Mills v. Nand Kishore (1956) II LLJ 439:AIR 1957 SC 7.*

The dismissal order of the employee was declared invalid in the absence of service of the show cause notice. *Paru Silk Mills Vikhroli v. Shamsuddin Abdulhuq, 1954 ICR 1047 (IC Bom.).*

Charge sheet is the initiating point of disciplinary action, which provides the basis for the domestic enquiry, as the charge need to be established or confirmed in the enquiry held for the purpose. It informs the charge-sheeted workman clearly, precisely and accurately of the omissions and commissions alleged against him. *Sur Enamel and Stamping Works Ltd. V. Workmen, 1993 II LLJ 367 (SC).*

Is charge-sheet a show cause letter, or can a show cause letter be treated as a charge sheet ?

Yes, every charge-sheet is a show-cause letter, but every show-cause letter may not be considered a charge-sheet.

A charge-sheet is a show cause letter. Firstly, the charge levelled against an employee in the charge-sheet is never considered final, and the employee is not held guilty on the basis of such accusation of charge. The charge needs to be proved in an enquiry. Secondly, the charge-sheet essentially provides opportunity to the charge-sheeted employee to provide a written explanation to the charge-sheet. If, the explanation given by the employee is found satisfactory by the disciplinary or charge-sheet issuing authority then the charge against the employee is liable to be dropped. The process of enquiry begins only after the explanation of the employee is found unsatisfactory and unacceptable by the charge-sheet issuing authority. Hence, a charge-sheet is always a show-cause letter.

If a show cause letter contains all the ingredients that a charge-sheet must contain then it can be considered a charge-sheet, otherwise not. If a show cause letter or an office memo is described as a charge-sheet, and it mentions the charges and asks the employee to show cause as to why he should not be suitably dealt with, then it cannot be argued that there was no charge-sheet considering a formal enquiry. *Krishna Chandra Tandon v. Union Of India (1974) 4 SCC 374.*

The Supreme Court has held that the charge must not contain any expression which would give rise to reasonable apprehension in the mind of the workman against whom the enquiry is held that the management has already made up its mind as to his guilt. *Powari Tea Estate v. M.K.Barktaki (1965 II LLJ 102).*

(a) Contents of a Charge-sheet, or, what should be mentioned in a charge- sheet

(i) A charge- sheet contains the particulars that are required to identify the person against whom the charge has been framed.

A charge-sheet should contain the specific details of the employee to whom it is issued. It contains name of the employee, specific identity number given to the employee by the organization, department, grade or designation of the employee or any other personal detail which is required to be mentioned as per the norms of the organization.

(ii) A charge-sheet contains date, time and place of occurrence.

A charge-sheet very specifically contains the date, time and place of misconduct committed by the employee. In absence of specific details regarding date, time and place of offence a charge-sheet becomes vague which can be invalidated.

The charge on an employee was that "you committed gross misconduct and insubordination by leaving your work place unattended and staged a meeting inside the factory during your working hours and despite orders continued to do so ". The charge was considered to be vague as it lacked particular date and time of incident. *Management of Jagjit Beverages v. Workmen, Delhi Government Gazette, Dt. 11.06.59, Part VI, P 250 (IT).*

When it is not possible to mention any specific date or time, for example when offence stretches over a period, it is sufficient to mention the period between which the offence was committed. It should be borne in mind that the purpose is to let the employee know of the offence for which he is charged.

(iii) A charge-sheet contains brief description of the charges

A charge-sheet contains brief description of the acts of omission or commission that constitute misconduct. The purpose of the charge-sheet is to clearly convey the employee the specific allegations or complaints that stand against him. A charged employee can properly prepare his defences only when he is aware about the act of omission or commission by him that constitute misconduct. Any unclear or incomplete description of charge is considered vague, and is liable to be invalidated. An act of punishment on the basis of vague charge stands bad in the eyes of the law.

If vague charge is given it is a fatal defect which vitiates the entire proceedings. *Avinash Chandra Sanjar v. Divl. Suptd. Central Railway, Jhansi (1962) I LLJ 7, 12 All (HC).*

An employee was charged that he accepted private work in a manner which robbed the company of its essential work. This was considered to be a vague charge. *Naidu S.V. v. Blackwoods (India) Ltd. (1957) 2 LLJ 340 (IC Nag.)*

The charges should contain full description and should be specific and not vague otherwise it will vitiate the enquiry proceedings. *Central Bank Of India v. Karunamoy Bannerjee, (1967) 2 LLJ 739;*

(iv) A charge-sheet contains relevant clauses and sub-clauses constituting misconduct

The clauses and sub-clauses relating to the misconduct as mentioned in rules and regulations for the employees of an organization or relating to the misconduct as mentioned in the Standing Orders of the Company are required to be mentioned in the charge-sheet.

The necessity of this provision is there because omission and commissions of acts that constitute misconduct are properly defined and communicated to the employees in every organization. Both, the employer as well as the employees, are aware that what acts of omission and commission would constitute a misconduct. It is also a requirement that Standing Orders of the Company should be displayed in the organization. As a matter of fact, vagueness should not be there in this respect as to what exactly constitutes a misconduct. Therefore, whenever an employee commits a misconduct the charge-sheet contains the specific provisions of the rule that are violated. An employee cannot claim ignorance about the misconduct.

However, a mere mention of the relevant clause and sub-clause defining misconduct in the absence of proper description of the actual charge committed by the employee is considered to be incomplete. *Govind S. Thakur v. Jagjit Distillery & Allied Industries Ltd., Delhi Admin. Gazette, 19.09.1963 p. 169.*

(v) A charge-sheet contains time limit for submission of explanation, in writing, to the charges

A charge-sheet mentions time limit within which the charged employee must submit his explanation, in writing, to the charges levelled against him. It is essential to provide the charged employee an opportunity to provide an explanation to the charges. A sufficient time must be given to the charge-sheeted employee to provide written explanation to the charge-sheet. The violation of this provision is considered a violation of the theory of natural justice.

When the charge-sheet did not mention that the workman had to give the explanation to the charge-sheet in writing, then it was considered to be defective. *Zhandu Pharmaceuticals v. Workmen, Mah. Gazette, dt. 14.07.1966 p.2217 (LC).*

Only when the reply or explanation to the charge-sheet submitted by the employee has been found unsatisfactory by the charge-sheet issuing authority then an enquiry should proceed. *Workmen v. Management of M/S Girson Mills, Punj. Gazette, dt. 07.10.1966 p. 1785 (LC).*

This does not, however, mean that there should be unreasonable waiting period for the reply of the charge-sheet by the employee. There may also be a probability that the charge-sheeted employee would refrain from giving any explanation for whatsoever reason.

Normally a period of forty eight to seventy two hours from the receipt of the charge-sheet or proper service of the charge-sheet is considered a sufficient time for reply of the charge-sheet by the employee. However, it also depends on specific case as to what would be appropriate time limit for reply of the charge-sheet. Geographical distance, mode of delivery available , time taken by postal service, complexity and comprehensiveness of the charges, requirement by the charge-sheeted employee to inspect any document or record before giving explanation of the charges etc. must be considered before providing a sufficient time-limit for providing written explanation to the charge-sheet by the employee.

Providing less than twenty four hours time to submit written explanation to the charge-sheet after the service of the charge-sheet contains a fatal defect in the charge-sheet. *City Transport Ltd., Coimbatore v. Workmen , (1952) I LLJ 457 (IT).*

The time limit mentioned in the Standing Orders or the Rules and Regulations of the service for reply of the charge-sheet by the delinquent employee must not be ignored and time limit should be granted accordingly. The employer should not seem to be in any haste in this regard.

It has been held by the Supreme Court that non-compliance of standing orders regarding time limit to be provided for giving explanation to the charge-sheet brings infirmity in the proceedings. *Management of Travancore Titanium Products v. Workmen, (1970) 2 LLJ I (SC).*

If the charge-sheeted employee requests on reasonable grounds for extension of time limit to provide written explanation then a reasonable extension of time should be granted. A reasonable time must be allowed to the charge-sheeted workman to provide explanation to the charge-sheet. Any denial of request for extension of time limit is held bad in the eyes of law. Whether sufficient opportunity was given or not would depend upon the facts of each case. *Bahadur Nanak v. Poddar Mills Ltd., Mah. Gaz. Dt. 02.04.1970. p. 1935.*

(vi) *A charge sheet contains information about suspension pending enquiry, if applicable.*

In serious nature of offence, and where the presence of the employee at the workplace can affect the enquiry procedure, an employee is kept suspended pending enquiry into the charge-sheet. The information about suspension must be properly informed to the delinquent employee and it is appropriate to mention the same in the charge-sheet.

It is also regular and flawless to forthwith suspend an employee on his commissioning a serious misconduct by issuing a simple official memo or letter to him keeping pending the issue of a formal charge-sheet to him. However, such suspension order must also be issued by appropriate authority only.

(Vii) Additional information that a charge-sheet may contain

A charge-sheet may also contain-

- Previous record of the employee of any offence committed by him in the past provided such offence was proved in a duly held enquiry where the employee had the opportunity to cross examine all the evidences and witnesses that held him guilty of the offence. The previous record is mentioned to exacerbate the charge.

- Statement of allegations or complaints if it is required to be mentioned for proper comprehension of the charges by the employee. In the absence of documents on which it is based, a charge-sheet can become vague and invalid. *Banaras Light & Power Co. Ltd., v. Bijlighar Mazdoor Sangh, (1952) I LLJ 6 (LAT).*

  When the charges are base it is all the more necessary to supply statement of allegations specially if it is demanded. *Suresh Chandra Chakravorty v. State of W.B. (1970) 3 SCC 548.*

- Information containing inspection of documents or records by the employee in case the charges are based on them, and it is necessary for the employee to inspect those documents or records to understand the charge levelled against him.

- A charge-sheet may also contain the proposed date of enquiry and name or names of the enquiry officer if it is clearly mentioned in the charge sheet that enquiry would proceed only when the explanation submitted by him is found unsatisfactory.

  The charge-sheet should also mention the place, date and time on which the delinquent workman should appear before the enquiry officer. *City Transport Ltd., Coimbatore v. Workmen, (1952) I LLJ 457 (IT).*

(b) What should a charge-sheet not contain, or what should not be mentioned in the charge-sheet

(i) A charge-sheet should not contain evidences

A charge-sheet is not supposed to be a record of evidence. If evidence is not mentioned in the charge-sheet a charge-sheet does not carry any infirmity. *New Victoria Mills Co. v. Jagannath, (1964) I LLJ 110 (All H.C.).*

A charge-sheet need not contain the names of witnesses or a list of documents on the basis of which charge has been made.

Maharashtra State Road Transport Corporation v. R.D. Tirhekar (Mah. Gaz., dt. 16.10.1966, p. 4980 (LC).

(ii) A charge-sheet should not contain proposed punishment

A charge-sheet is not required to mention proposed penalty in the charge-sheet. It may prejudice the enquiry officer, and thus, vitiate the enquiry. It may also be taken to mean that the disciplinary authority has already taken a decision about the punishment and the enquiry is a mere formality. It may, therefore, vitiate the enquiry. *Gouri Prasad Ghosh v. State of W.B., (1968) Lab IC 735 (Cal H.C.)*

If punishment is mentioned in the charge-sheet then it is invalid. *Ram Gopal Nigam v. State of U.P. 1968 Lab IC 1476 (All H.C.).*

The authority to decide punishment should not determine any punishment even before the charges are established. *Khem Chand v. Union of India AIR, 1958 SC 300.*

(iii) A charge-sheet should not contain abbreviations.

A charge-sheet should not contain abbreviations which is not capable of being understood ordinarily. Only specific details should be mentioned in the charge-sheet.

(c) Who should issue a charge-sheet

The employer or the appointing authority has the right to take disciplinary action against the employee. A charge-sheet which is issued by the employer or the appointing authority cannot carry a defect regarding authority to issue a charge-sheet. But, in any Company or Organization not essentially all the employees work directly under the employer or the appointing authority. The management system of any Company or Organization creates different authorities invested with certain powers to run the system of management. In disciplinary matters relating to employees certain powers are delegated based on hierarchy of the system. Some authorities are invested with the power to initiate disciplinary proceedings, some authorities are invested with the powers to award certain punishments. It all depends on the delegation of authority.

Only the disciplinary authority that has been invested with the powers to initiate disciplinary proceedings can issue a charge-sheet and initiate disciplinary action. A charge-sheet issued by an incompetent authority makes the charge-sheet invalid. A disciplinary action cannot be taken on the basis on an invalid charge-sheet.

A Charge-sheet is not a record of evidence. The person signing the charge-sheet i.e., the disciplinary authority is not accuser. He does not hold himself responsible for the truth of the facts mentioned in the charge-sheet. It remains to be proved in an enquiry to be held for the purpose.

In the absence of proper delegation of administrative powers relating to employee if any authority initiates disciplinary actions against an employee then the employee can raise a question of inappropriateness of the action and invasion on his fundamental rights. *Shardul Singh v. State Of M.P. AIR 1966 MP 193.*

Only an authority competent to initiate disciplinary action against an employee can issue a charge-sheet. Whenever the disciplinary authority, whether in private or public sector, or government organization, receives a complaint against the employee, the disciplinary authority takes a decision to properly frame the charges to be issued to the delinquent employee. Regarding the public servants the provisions mentioned in The Public Servants (Inquiries) Act, 1850 reads as hereunder:

Articles of Charge to be drawn out for public enquiry into conduct of certain public servants:

Whenever the Government shall be of opinion that there are good ground for making a formal and public enquiry into the truth of any imputation of misbehaviour by any person in the service of the Government, not removable from his appointment without the sanction of the government, it may cause the substance of the imputation to be drawn into distinct articles of charge and may order a formal and public enquiry to be made into the truth thereof.

It is abundant duty of the disciplinary authority to frame charges against a delinquent employee immediately on receiving a complaint.

(d) *Language of the Charge-sheet*

A Charge-sheet is normally written in English. It is also bi-lingual, sometimes, and translation is mentioned in a vernacular language, which is understood by majority of the workmen employed in the establishment. However, a charge-sheet issued in English language only is not considered imperfect. *Tractors India Ltd. v. Mohammad Sayeed, AIR 1959, SC 1196.*

(e) When should a charge-sheet be issued

A charge-sheet should be issued by the disciplinary authority on receiving complaint against a delinquent employee without any unreasonable delay.

If on receiving a complaint against an employee a charge-sheet is not issued promptly then it may indicate that (i) the disciplinary authority is not working impartially (ii) the disciplinary authority has condoned the charge, or (iii) the disciplinary authority may act vindictively at a latter point of time when the employee will not be left with enough memory to sufficiently provide an explanation.

A delay of about one and a half year is fatal and does not afford reasonable opportunity to show cause. *M.D.Parmar v. Y.B.Zala, (1980) I LLJ 260 (Guj. H.C.).*

(f) How is a charge-sheet served

A charge-sheet is served to the delinquent employee in the presence of two independent witnesses. Independent witness means they should not be related to the case. Receiving of the employee is taken on a copy of the charge-sheet along with the attestation of the independent witnesses. *This is the first course of action for service of the charge-sheet.*

The delinquent employee , on occasions , applies several tricks indirectly to avoid receiving the charge-sheet. He can even openly refuse to accept the charge-sheet. The second course of action is to post the charge-sheet on the departmental notice board and along with it copies of the charge-sheet are sent by registered post with acknowledgement due to the known residential addresses, temporary and permanent, of the employee as mentioned in the official records. *This is the second course of action for proper service of the charge-sheet.*

The delinquent employee often deliberately not receives the charge-sheet sent by post, or sometimes the address also may not be correct. In that event, the charge-sheet is required to be published in two local newspapers. *This third course of action is considered as final and proper service of the charge-sheet.*

Even then, if the delinquent employee does not appear for the enquiry, the enquiry in that case proceeds, ex-parte, in the absence of the delinquent employee, without any procedural defect.

(g) *Refusal to accept the charge-sheet is considered a misconduct*

Refusal to accept charge-sheet by the employee is considered a misconduct as it is disobedience and an act subversive of discipline. Sometimes, refusal to accept a charge-sheet is mentioned as a separate misconduct in the Standing Orders of the Company. When refusal to accept charge-sheet is treated as a misconduct then a separate charge-sheet is required to be issued for the purpose, and accordingly a separate enquiry is constituted.

Refusal to accept charge-sheet is also a gross indiscipline and a deliberate and calculated attempt to interfere in the working of the office. *Atherton West and Co. Ltd. v. Regional Conciliation Officer, AIR 1959 All 406.*

(h) Format of a charge-sheet

There is no specific format for a charge-sheet. The charge(s) can be mentioned in a simple letter or in a properly formatted charge-sheet. To avoid deviations and discrepancies a format of the charge-sheet is often kept in the organization and the same format is used each time when there is a need to issue a charge-sheet.

A format of charge-sheet has been mentioned at the end of chapter VI.

CHANCE WITNESS

A chance witness is a witness who should not normally be where and when he professes to have been. If a person is at the place of occurrence and witnesses an incident by chance, then he is considered to be a chance witness.

The testament of a chance witness is equally important. The evidence of a chance witness is not necessarily incredible or unbelievable. It requires close scrutiny. In industrial or departmental enquiry very often chance witnesses are less relied upon and unless and until the witness gives any plausible reason for his presence at a place by chance, or his witness is not corroborated by other witnesses, his witness is considered to be ignored without any indignation.

However, the testimony of a witness should not become unacceptable on the grounds of his being a chance witness. *Brij Bhushan v. State, AIR 1955 (NUC) ll 6042.*

COMPULSORY RETIREMENT

Compulsory retirement simpliciter is not considered as punishment. It is done in 'public interest' and does not caste a stigma on the Government servant. So the employee cannot claim an opportunity to be heard before he is compulsorily retired from service. The Supreme Court of India has issued certain guidelines regarding compulsory retirement. Compulsory retirement shall not be imposed as a punitive measure. In *Baikunth Nath v Chief Medical Officer(1992),2 SCC 299,* the Court issued clarifications regarding compulsory retirement.

(i)   The order of compulsory retirement is not a punishment. It implies no stigma.

(ii) The order has to be passed by the government in public interest. The order is passed on the subjective satisfaction of the government.

(iii) Principles of natural justice have no place in the context of an order of compulsory retirement. However courts will interfere if the order is passed *mala fide* or there is no evidence or it is arbitrary.

(iv) The government shall have to consider the entire record of service before taking a decision in the matter particularly during the later years' record and performance.

(v)   An order of compulsory retirement is not liable to be quashed by a Court merely on showing that while passing it excommunicated adverse remarks were taken into consideration. The circumstances by itself cannot be a basis for interference.

In State of Gujarat v *Umedbhai M. Patel, AIR 2001 SC 1109,* the Court laid further down the following principles.

(a) When the Service of a public servant is no longer useful to the general administration, the officer can be compulsorily retired in public interest.

(b) Ordinarily an order of compulsory retirement is not to be treated as a punishment under Art. 311 of the Constitution.

(c) For better administration, it is necessary to chop off dead wood but the order of compulsory retirement can be based after having due regard to the entire service record of the officer.

(d) Any adverse entries made in the confidential record shall be taken note of and be given due weightage in passing such order.

(e) Even uncommunicated entries in the confidential report can also be taken in to consideration.

(f) The order of compulsory retirement shall not be passed as a short cut to avoid departmental inquiry when such course is more desirable.

(g) If the officer is given promotion despite adverse entries in the C. R., that is a fact in favour of the officer.

In private enterprises also compulsory retirement is a glorified procedure of terminating services of an executive whose services are no more useful for the enterprise. The more common terminology used in case of private enterprise in this regard is 'termination simpliciter'.

CONFESSION

A confession is a statement by a suspect in any crime against law, or any misconduct of offence in violation of any rule, which is adverse to that person. Confession evidence can be considered, arguably, the best piece of evidence of guilt; provided no duress is claimed by the suspect for making that confessionary statement. A confession statement must be made without any external pressure.

Confession has not been defined in the Indian Evidence Act. The word "confession" appears for the first time in section 24 of the Indian Evidence Act. This section comes under the heading of 'Admission' purporting confession to be merely one species of admission.

Confession if deliberately and voluntarily made may be accepted as conclusive of the matters confessed. Whereas, 'Admissions' are not conclusive as the matters admitted. It may, however, operate as an *'estoppel' (estoppel is the principle which precludes a person from asserting something contrary to what is implied by a previous action statement of that Person).*

CO-WORKER

A co-worker is a person who helps the charge-sheeted employee at the enquiry in case the charge-sheeted employee is ignorant about the disciplinary proceedings, or even otherwise he needs assistance in this regard.

The Model Standing Order also contains the provision that a co-worker may be allowed at the enquiry.

The workman may take the assistance of a co-worker to help him in the enquiry, if he so desires. ***Industrial Employment (Standing Orders) , Central Rules, 1946.***

The choice of getting a co-worker lies with the charge-sheeted employee. At the beginning of the enquiry the charge sheeted employee is given opportunity to seek assistance of a co-worker at the enquiry. A co-worker, if allowed by the enquiry officer, as per rules, to assist the delinquent employee in the enquiry, is released by the management from work to attend the enquiry sessions. Normally, the standing orders of a company or the rules and regulations of an organization mentions the policy as to who can be allowed as a co-worker in enquiry proceedings.

If the charge-sheeted employee refuses to take assistance of any co-worker at the enquiry then this fact should be properly documented in the proceedings, and the signature of the charge-sheeted employee is taken to affirm this fact, along with the signature of other concerned persons present at the enquiry. This is done with a view so that the charge-sheeted employee should not later claim that he was not allowed to avail this reasonable and lawful opportunity.

A co-worker is a fellow worker of the charge-sheeted employee who preferably works in the same department or work area where the delinquent employee works. The Model Standing Order mentions that a co-worker can be an office-bearer of the Union to which the employee is associated.

In the enquiry, the workman shall be entitled to appear in person or to be represented by an office-bearer of a trade union of which he is a member. *Industrial Employment (Standing Orders) , Central Rules, 1946.*

Whether an employee can be allowed to be represented by an advocate in the enquiry proceedings depends on the rules and regulations of the organization or provisions contained in the Standing Orders of the Company as also the circumstances of the case. The scale should always be evenly balanced so that an employee facing the charge is not put to any inconvenience in furthering his case.

The law does not confer an absolute right of representation on the employee in domestic enquiries as part of his rights to be heard and there is no right to representation by somebody else unless the relevant rules or regulations and standing orders specifically recognize such a right and provide for such representation. *Indian Overseas Bank v. Indian Overseas Bank Officer's Association, 2001 9 SCC 540.*

DISCHARGE

Discharge is severing the contract of employment for an employee by an action of the management which may be due to multiple reasons. However, when an employee is discharged from the services after the misconduct of the employee is duly proved at the domestic enquiry, it is a punishment. It is the discretion of the employer to either dismiss or discharge a delinquent employee once his guilts are proved at the enquiry. Discharge is considered a less severe punishment in comparison to dismissal.

Discharge simply means termination of service under the contract of employment. In case of discharge the workman is entitled to notice or wages in lieu of it. Generally, the employment letter issued by the employer contains one clause which reads like *"The employment is liable to be terminated at any time by giving one/three month's notice, or wages in lieu of notice, by either side."* This simply means that the employer reserves the right to terminate the services of the employee, and the employee can also resign and quit the service.

The employer can terminate the service and discharge an employee on the simple ground of 'loss of faith' on an employee. However, 'loss of faith' carries an stigma for the employee. Therefore, an opportunity should be given to employee by the employer to put his case vis-à-vis employer's charge of loss of faith on him before the discharge is effected. Contrarily, an employee can also severe the contract of employment for his own reasons. Ideally, a resignation must also contain reasons for leaving the services of an employer.

Discharge Simpliciter: When an employer terminates the services of an employee invoking the simple clause of termination of service giving notice or wages in lieu of notice, as mentioned above, it is called 'discharge simpliciter'. Examples of discharge simpliciter are 'strucking off the name of an employee from the muster rolls of the establishment if he has not presented himself for duty for a fairly long period', 'non-renewal of the contract of service for an employee' etc. Discharge simpliciter is also called as 'termination simpliciter'.

No enquiry is required for Simple Discharge or Termination of Service

Simple discharge or termination of service does not require any enquiry. An enquiry is required only in case of punishment. Article

311 of the Constitution is also not required in case of a simple termination of service which is not effected by way of punishment. *B. S. Srivastava v. Collector & Distt. Magistrate, Jaunpur, (1961) 2 LLJ 191: AIR 1961 All 284.*

In government service an employee holds a contract of service practically till he attains the age or superannuation or when the contract of service is severed by the employee by resignation of service or voluntary retirement. If the termination of service is effected by a decision of the Government then prima facie it constitutes punishment. *Purushottam Lal Dhingra v. Union of India, AIR 1958 SC 36.*

Simple Discharge or Termination of service should be in accordance with Rules

An employee can be discharged from service by invoking the related clauses in the letter of employment or the rules and regulations in this regard. When the rules provide that a particular authority has the power to terminate the services but no specific procedure has been laid down in relation thereto then there is no lack of competence to pass order of termination. *Padmanav Sipka v. Chairman Notified Area Council, Kantabanji, 1973 SLJ 1026 (1974) I LLJ 69 (Ori HC).*

Termination of service in pursuance of service rules or agreement is different from dismissal or removal from service. *Shyamlal v. State of U.P. AIR 1954 SC 369; Purushottam Lal Dhingra v. Union of India, AIR 1958 SC 36.*

Discharge or Termination of Service in breach of Standing Orders or Rules of the Organization is invalid

An employer must discharge any employee working under him according to rules and regulations of the organization as mentioned in the Service Rules of the Organization or the Standing Orders. The termination of service in breach of Standing Orders in invalid. *Tata Chemicals Limited v. Workmen, AIR 1964, Guj. 265.*

Discharge Constructive or Constructive Discharge: Constructive discharge occurs when an employee claims that his working conditions were made so intolerable that he was forced to quit.

In constructive discharge an employee is forced to resign due to actions and conditions becoming so intolerable or aggravated that a reasonable person in the employee's position would normally resign. The employer of the employee in such cases, is in full knowledge of the conditions under which the employee resigns, but he does not take any step to remedy the condition.

In other words, when an employer pushes an employee to resign and quit work it is called constructive discharge.

The factors that contribute to constructive discharge are –

- Demotion
- Reduction in Salary
- Reduction in job responsibilities
- Assignment to work under younger supervisor
- Involuntary transfer to a less desirable place or position
- Badgering, harassment or humiliation by the employer
- Threat of violence or actual physical assault
- Threat of termination
- Initiating disciplinary action on flimsy grounds

DISMISSAL

Dismissal is the ultimate punishment that can be inflicted on an employee by the employer. The punishment of dismissal is awarded when the act of misconduct is very serious, or when an employee commits misconduct repeatedly and does not show any sign of correction in his behavior. An incorrigible employee who frequently creates problems relating to discipline in the organization becomes a liability for the employer. The punishment of dismissal is often justified in such cases. An employee whose previous past record is good then he can be lightly dealt with by the employer. *Narayan Amar v. Rajkumar Mills Ltd., 1960 I LLJ 654 (IT)*. But, a person who commits misconduct repeatedly does not deserve any grace and can be dismissed by the employer.

Dismissal ends the employment contract in a very unpleasant manner. It leaves an stigma or scar on the career of an employee. It also results in injury to the feelings and sentiments of the employee. It affects the future prospects of the employee. Dismissal also affects the employee in financial terms. His terminal benefits like gratuity, and employer's part of PF may be denied.

Dismissal also affects the employer. It has the potential to give rise to serious industrial relations problems. Besides, the employer may face a long drawn court case which is no less nagging. Therefore, an order of dismissal must be passed by with care and caution. When a workman is dismissed then justice, equity and good conscience demand that he should not be dismissed perfunctorily and a high officer should apply his mind to the case. *Indian Iron and Steel Co. Ltd., v. Workmen Cal. Gaz., Part I C , dt. 26.12.1968 p. 1445 (IT).*

Who should issue a dismissal order

A dismissal order may be issued by the employer himself or an authority who has been properly delegated powers in this regard to pass such an order.

A dismissal order issued by an incompetent authority is wholly null and void and, therefore, it can never be validated. *M.M. Siddiqui v. Union of India ,AIR 1965, All 568; Ishwar Narain v. Union Of India, AIR 1957, All 439.*

A competent authority should himself pass the dismissal order or give his consent in writing after considering the appropriateness of the case. A mere previous sanction of the competent authority cannot be presumed to be an order of dismissal passed by that authority. *T.C. Nilamegham Pillai v. Secretary of State, AIR, 1937 Mad. 777.* In the absence of proper delegation of administrative powers if an order of dismissal is passed by a subordinate authority then it is null and void, or invalid.

When Should the dismissal order be passed

A dismissal order should be passed when the guilt of the employee has been duly proved in a fair and impartial enquiry. The appropriate punishing authority should properly consider the findings of the enquiry officer, and pass an order of dismissal after giving the employee an opportunity to represent his case as to why his misconduct should not be punished by an order of dismissal. The Punishing authority should give reasons for his arriving at a decision to award dismissal order. The reply of the delinquent employee should be properly considered before awarding the final order of dismissal.

What should the dismissal order contain

A dismissal order should contain the charge or charges leading to dismissal and the effective date of dismissal. A dismissal order cannot be retrospective. However, if it is properly mentioned in

Rules of the Organization or Standing Orders of a Company then the date of suspension of the employee pending enquiry proceedings can become the effective date of dismissal.

The Dismissal Order should be in writing, and should contain charges

An order of dismissal must be in writing and must state the reason or charge for which the delinquent employee is dismissed. A worker cannot be dismissed for misconduct for he was not charged. A worker can be dismissed only for a charge which has been duly proved in a fair and impartial enquiry. *K. S. Rao v. State of A.P. AIR 1957 A.P. 414.*

Mere technical errors in dismissal order does not invalidate the dismissal order if it is issued by appropriate authority and correctly mentions the charges which have been proved.

A dismissal order without an enquiry is not void

A dismissal order without an enquiry is not void. It is not necessary that a dismissal order will be declared void merely because the charge has not been proved in a duly constituted domestic or departmental enquiry. The merits of the dismissal order is always subject to review by the Tribunal. *Punjab National Bank v. Punjab National Bank Employees' Federation, AIR, 1960, SC, 160, 173.*

For the employees in the civil services of the Government or the State a disciplinary order of dismissal may not be essentially preceded by an enquiry. Article 311 of the constitution mentions that -

where the authority empowered to dismiss or remove a person or to reduce him in rank is satisfied that for some reason, to be recorded by that authority in writing, it is not reasonably practicable to hold such inquiry; or where the President or the Governor, as the case may be, is satisfied that in the interest of the security of the State, it is not expedient to hold such inquiry then the decision thereon of the authority empowered to dismiss or remove such person or to reduce him in rank shall be final.

It is the merit of a case that justifies a dismissal. However, the decision of not holding an enquiry should be based on sound reasons because the decision of the employer to dismiss the employee is always subject to judicial review. The dismissed employee can challenge in the law court the act of dismissal holding it as arbitrary and unfair.

Disciplinary Authority should take suggestion where required before passing dismissal order:

If the disciplinary authority is required to take suggestion from any authority be it mandatory or discretionary, the rules and regulations mentioned in this regard or any constitutional or statutory provision relating thereto must not be ignored else the decision may become invalid and infirm. Article 320 (3) (c) of the Constitution of India mentions that- The Union Public Service Commission or State Public Service Commission shall be consulted in all disciplinary matters affecting a person working under the Government of India or the Government of State in civil capacity including memorials or petitions relating to such matters and it shall be duty of the Public Service Commission to advise on any matter so referred to them and on any other matter which the President or the Governor of the State, as the case may be, may refer to them, and incase the Public Service Commission is consulted in any matter of disciplinary matter then the records of the enquiry together with the second show cause notice, if any, and reply thereto are sent to the Public Service Commission before taking final action on the matter.

If the Standing Orders of any Company require that any particular authority is to be consulted before passing any dismissal order then the provision of the Standing Orders must be followed because the Standing Order also contains statutory sanction since it is based on statutory obligation.

The Courts have, however, given different verdicts, based on merits of the case, regarding validity of dismissal order passed by the Government vis-a-vis consultation by the Public Service Commission on the matter.

Dismissal Order is not passed when an employee is in sick leave

An employee is not dismissed when he is in sick leave. Section 73 of the Employees' State Insurance Act prohibits an employer from dismissing, discharging, reducing or punishing an employee when he is in receipt of sickness, maternity or disablement benefit or is under medical treatment for sickness. The reason is that the decision of such order of dismissal may adversely affect the health of the employee.

This rule is followed in case of employees not covered under the Employees' State Insurance Act, as well.

Difference between Discharge and Dismissal of an employee

The following are the major differences between discharge and dismissal of an employee:

1. Discharge is not essentially a punishment. Dismissal is essentially a punishment.
2. In discharge case of a disciplinary action the termination benefits are not withheld. In dismissal cases as a result of disciplinary action termination benefits like gratuity, employer's part of PF may be withheld.
3. Discharge is a less harsh action of an employer. Dismissal is considered a harsh punishment.

DEMOTION

An employee is said to be demoted when he is downgraded from the present job and is reduced to a lower cadre of service. This punishment is somewhat analogous to *"reduction in rank"* as envisaged by Article 311 of the Constitution of India.

When the increments are stopped with future effect then it amounts to permanent reduction in the stage of progress and it constitutes reduction in rank. The Supreme Court has held that reduction has reference to classification and must involve reduction to lower post or lower time scale. Reduction to a stage in the same time scale does not amount to reduction in rank. *High Court of Calcutta v. Amal Kumar Roy, AIR 1962 SC 1704.*

The reduction in rank or demotion, in effect, is a very serious punishment where the contract of service does not end and the employee is obliged to work with loss of face and humiliation. Often an employee prefers discharge or termination to demotion. Conversely, an intended termination can be wrapped in notice of demotion.

An employer terminated the service of the employee but considering the past record, offered him a job on same salary and fixed a date for his exercising option for the job. The employee did not exercise the option. The labour court held that the order of termination was in fact an order of demotion and ordered further enquiry on the question whether the order was mollified. The High Court observed that as the employee did not avail himself of the option, his services had ended after the appointed date of exercising the option. Hence the order was not considered as the order of demotion, but was an actual termination of service. *National Engineering Employees Union V.R.N. Kulkarni, (1968) II LLJ 82 Bombay (DB)*.

DOMESTICS ENQUIRY

Domestic Enquiry is a 'qusi-judicial' activity. When an enquiry is done in the organization by the officials employed therein at the instance of the employer (management) to find the veracity of allegation of misconduct levelled against an employee, in common parlance it is called 'domestic or departmental enquiry'. An Enquiry Officer is appointed by the disciplinary authority who enquires into the charge of misconduct levelled against an employee of the organization. An officer appointed by the management, often called Presenting Officer or Management Representative, is given the responsibility to prove the charge against the delinquent employee by leading 'prosecution witnesses' in the enquiry. The charged employee presents witnesses and evidences from his side called, 'defence witnesses'. Each side is given opportunity to cross examine the witnesses of the other side. At the end of the enquiry the Enquiry Officer prepares a report of the enquiry based on the evidences on record and submits the same to the disciplinary authority. Technically, a domestic or departmental enquiry commences with framing of the charge-sheet and concludes when the Enquiry Officer submits the enquiry report to the Disciplinary Authority.

The terms domestic and departmental enquiry are same. The thin line of difference is that the term 'departmental enquiry' is used more frequently for government employees, and 'domestic enquiry' is more frequently used in case of industrial and commercial employees. For employees working in government or semi-government organizations "Service Terms" or "Service Rules" are applicable. However, the terms and conditions of service for industrial or commercial employees are mentioned in the Standing Orders of the industry or commercial undertaking which is framed as per Industrial Employment (Standing Orders) Act, 1946. Provisions relating to disciplinary action on the public servants have been mentioned in Article 311 of the Constitution. Besides, the Public Servants Enquiries Act, 1850 is also present in statute book.

Whether in private enterprise or public sector or any government organization, the domestic or departmental enquiry is guided by the rules of natural justice which ensures justice, impartiality and fair play in domestic enquiry.

Domestic enquiry is similar to a trial in a court of law that is why it is called a 'quasi-judicial' activity. But, while a trial in a court of law is for crimes done against society, domestic enquiry is conducted for offences committed against the establishment for misconduct punishable under the Standing Orders or Rule and Regulations of the Organization. The difference between domestic enquiry and trial in a court is that the Evidence Act is not applicable in case of domestic enquiry, and the enquiry officer, like a judge in courts of law, cannot summon witnesses in a domestic enquiry. Moreover, the enquiry officer in a domestic enquiry cannot pronounce penalty or punishment, unless the final disciplinary authority himself acts as an enquiry officer.

The need for domestic enquiry lies in the fact that any offender should be punished following the rules of natural justice. There should not be any arbitrariness in awarding punishment to employees for their alleged acts of misconduct. It also restricts the employers to award punishment to employees on their whims and fancy.

The process of domestic enquiry creates a balance of power. The employees cannot disturb the discipline inside the organization because a disciplinary procedure acts like a check which ensures orderliness in the organization. At the same time, the employers cannot punish employees arbitrarily because a delinquent employee must be punished according to rules, and only after confirmation of his alleged act of misconduct in a free and fair enquiry. A plethora of case laws established over a considerable length of time has made it obligatory for the employers to conduct a fair and unbiased enquiry before awarding any punishment to it's employee.

Discharge or dismissal of an employee without holding a fair and unbiased domestic enquiry, in accordance with the theories of natural justice, is frowned upon by labour courts and tribunals. An employee who is wrongly dismissed is liable to be reinstated at the intervention of the Courts. It is very much essential, therefore, to hold fair and unbiased enquiry to inflict punishment to any delinquent employee. Article 311 of the Constitution of India lays emphasis on the need of such enquiry in case of employees working under the service of the State. The Standing Orders Act makes the provision for employees working in industrial and commercial undertakings.

The mere fact that an enquiry has been conducted will not satisfy the requirements of industrial adjudication to validate the disciplinary action against a workman. It will be presumed that an enquiry has not been committed unless-

(a) The delinquent has been informed clearly of the charges levelled against him.

(b) All the witnesses and material facts are brought at the enquiry, and the delinquent employee gets a fair opportunity to cross-examine them.

(c) The delinquent employee is given fair opportunity to defend himself and present facts and witnesses to prove himself innocent.

(d) The enquiry officer, an independent and unbiased person, records his findings with reasons for the same in his report.

It may be mentioned that conducting domestic enquiry is not just a formality. It is an essential condition to the legality of the disciplinary action. It should not be reduced to an empty formality. A case of 'defective enquiry' is equated with a case of 'no enquiry', and in such case the Tribunal would have the jurisdiction to go into the facts, and in such case the employer would have to satisfy on facts that the dismissal or discharge was correct and properly executed. *Workmen of Firestone Tyre and Rubber Co. of India Ltd vs Management 1975 – I LLJ – 278 (SC).*

In *Motipur Sugar Factory Case, (1965) 2 LLJ 162 27 FJR 376: AIR 1965 SC 1803,* the Supreme Court tried to clarify 'domestic enquiry' versus 'no enquiry' cases. The Apex Court stated that it should not be understood as laying down that there is no obligation whatsoever on the part of the employer to hold an enquiry before passing an order of discharge or dismissal.

In support of the requirement for holding an enquiry, the Court enumerated four basic reasons which can be mentioned as below-

(a) In spite of wider powers of adjudication now, the tribunal will have to give cogent reasons for not accepting the conclusions of the enquiry officer in a case where a proper enquiry has been held and a correct finding is arrived at regarding the misconduct of the workman.

(b) It will also enable the employer to persuade the tribunal to accept the enquiry as proper and the finding as correct.

(c) By holding a proper enquiry the employer will escape the charge of arbitrary action and *mala fide* intention.

(d) The holding of a proper and valid enquiry will conduce to the harmonious and healthy relations between the employer and the workmen. It will also foster industrial peace.

Domestic Enquiry has been dealt in more detail in chapter VI.

ENQUIRY OFFICER

The disciplinary procedure requires that the disciplinary authority will appoint an enquiry officer for conducting an enquiry into a case of misconduct to decide the guilt of an alleged charge-sheeted employee. The enquiry officer is always supposed to be an independent person who is unconnected with the case in which he is appointed an enquiry officer. An enquiry officer conducts domestic or departmental enquiry as per disciplinary procedure following the rules of natural justice. After conducting the enquiry the enquiry officer hands over the report of enquiry along with his findings and enquiry proceedings to the disciplinary authority who had appointed him as enquiry officer. The enquiry officer does not decide on or prescribe any punishment. The award of punishment is made by the disciplinary authority.

An enquiry Officer follows Rules of Natural Justice during enquiry

The rules of natural justice guides the enquiry officer during the enquiry proceedings in the absence of any procedural law. If the rules of natural justice is not followed at any stage during the enquiry procedure then the enquiry becomes bad in the eyes of the law.

The Principles of natural justice demand that the officer making enquiry should not be interested in bringing home the guilt to the accused at any cost. *Chakravorty v. Union of India AIR 1956 Cal 662.*

An enquiry officer is supposed to be neutral and unbiased.

An enquiry officer is supposed to be neutral and unbiased. He should not cross examine any witness in the enquiry. In the case of *Abdul Wajeed v. State of Karnataka, 1981(1) SLR 454 (Kar.)*, dealing with the validity of the enquiry where Enquiry Officer had cross-examined the defence witnesses, held, that the cross-examination of defence witnesses by the Enquiry Officer was in plain violation of the principles of natural justice and consequently the enquiry proceedings were vitiated.

An enquiry officer should never assume the role of Presenting Officer

An enquiry officer is appointed by the management to enquire into a case of misconduct by any employee of the Company. Although the enquiry officer is himself a part and parcel of management, but he is supposed to be neutral and unbiased. He cannot be expected to play the role of a presenter of management's viewpoint. A separate presenting officer is to be appointed by the disciplinary authority to present the case of the management. In the case of *C. Nagaraja Bhat v. Canara Bank, 1987(3) Kar. L.J. 232,* dealing with the effect of non-appointment of Presenting Officer and cross-examination of defence witnesses by Enquiring Authority itself, the Courts held that conduct of the enquiry in the absence of a Presentation Officer by the enquiry authority, as if he was the Presentation Officer, was clearly opposed to the rules of natural justice and fair-play.

Role of an Enquiry Officer

The Court very well defined the role of Enquiry officer in the case of Radhakrishna Setty. The Court in *Radhakrishna Setty v. Deputy General Manager (Disciplinary Authority), Indian Overseas Bank, Central Office, Madras,* has held that in a departmental proceedings, Enquiry Officer is an important person. When he is the key person, on him depends whether the enquiry would be fair or impartial. No doubt, the inquiry officer does not function like a Court and its proceedings also cannot be equated with the proceedings of the Court. Further, strict rules of Indian Evidence Act would not apply to its proceedings but certainly the principles which are based on the rules of natural justice would definitely apply. Certainly the Enquiry Officer may obtain all information, material for the points under enquiry from all sources and through all channels without being fettered by rules and procedure which govern the proceedings in the Court. The only obligation which the law casts upon them while eliciting the truth cannot go beyond the limit as an Enquiry Officer and play the role of a Prosecutor giving an indication that he was not fair and that he was biased. In the present case the Enquiry Officer himself had questioned the management witnesses and got all the documents marked in support of the allegations in the charge memo. After closing the Examination-in-Chief and the cross-examination of the witnesses by the defence representative, re-examines the witnesses which he characterizes as clarification. What is much more strange is that he goes beyond his scope to cross-examine the witnesses of the delinquent officer and assumes the role of Presenting Officer and a Prosecutor.

An enquiry Officer need not follow strict rules of Court of Law

Enquiry officers are not courts and, therefore, they are not bound to follow the procedure prescribed by the Trial Courts nor are they bound by strict rules of evidence. Their only obligations are those which the law casts on them. Namely; they should not take any action on information which they receive, unless they put it to the party against whom it is to be used and give him a fair opportunity to explain it. *State of Mysore v. Shivabasappa Shivappa, (1964 ILLJ SC, per Venkatrama Ayyar)*

The role of enquiry officer will be dealt in detail in chapter IV.

EVIDENCE

All documents including electronic records produced for the inspection of the court or at a quasi-judicial enquiry are called evidence. Evidence is every type of proof presented at the trial or enquiry which is intended to convince the judge of alleged facts related to or material to the case. An evidence is simply a document, data sheet or material proof that is brought at the enquiry in support of the statement of allegation by the management or in support of innocence that is brought by the delinquent. Evidences are displayed at the enquiry and properly exhibited by the enquiry officer. Material objects brought at the enquiry (theft material recovered etc.) are properly exhibited and documented in the enquiry proceedings and are given back to the investigating officer or presenting officer to be kept in safe custody for any future reference or production.

Sophisticated rules of evidence are not applicable in domestic enquiry

In the case of *State of Haryana v. Rattan Singh (1982 ILLJ 46 SC)*, the bench of three judges of the Supreme Court held that "It is well settled that in a domestic enquiry, strict and sophisticated rules of evidence under the Evidence Act may not apply. All materials which are logically probative for a prudent mind are permissible. There is no allergy to hearsay evidence provided; it has reasonable nexus and credibility." Simple laws of evidence are applicable in domestic enquiry.

Evidence which are relied upon for proving guilt must be displayed at enquiry

But, the principle that a fact sought to be proved must be supported by statements made in the presence of the person against whom the enquiry is held and that statements made behind the back of the person charged are not to be treated as substantive evidence, is one of the basic principles which cannot be ignored on the mere ground that domestic tribunals are not bound by the technical rules contained in the Evidence Act - *Central Bank of India Ltd. V. Prakash Chand Jain (1969) II LLJ 377 SC. The fundamental rules of Evidence Act are applicable in domestic enquiry.*

Evidence has been dealt in Chapter V in detail.

EXHIBIT

Exhibit is a document or thing produced for the inspection of the court, or shown to a witness when giving evidence or referred to in deposition. Exhibit in literal sense simply means 'to put on display', 'to put in view', 'to reveal'. All the documents, records, material evidence (i.e, all material objects) that are relied on by the management to prove the charges on the delinquent must be brought at the enquiry, and must be shown to the charge-sheeted employee at the enquiry. The simple theory of natural justice here is that charges cannot be proved on the delinquent on the basis of any hidden record, document or fact. The delinquent must get opportunity to see and question the document, record or material objects that are used against him. Likewise, the delinquent also gets opportunity to present all records, documents, material objects in his possession to present them at the enquiry to prove his innocence.

It is duty of the enquiry officer to document properly and serially the exhibits that are brought at the enquiry and properly get signature of all those present at the enquiry.

Failure to properly record and mention the exhibits may affect the enquiry adversely.

EXAMINATION-IN- CHIEF

Examination-in-chief is the questioning of a witness by the party which calles that witness to give evidence, in support of the case being made. The goals of the examination-in-chief are (a) to prove the elements to support the cause of action through the facts as deposed by a witness (b) to establish the credibility of a witness and, ultimately, the case itself (c) to lay the foundation to properly introduce exhibits into evidence.

EX-PARTE ENQUIRY

In case of *ex-parte* enquiry only one side is present. The proceedings of the enquiry is conducted in the absence of the other party. It is presumed that the other party is present. Each step of the enquiry is followed.

Domestic enquiry is also sometimes conducted in the absence of the delinquent employee. Despite several communications (normally three proper communications) made, if the delinquent employee does not present himself for the enquiry then the enquiry proceeds ex-parte. Proper opportunity for defence, as also proper communication of such opportunity, must be assured by the Enquiry Officer before conducting the enquiry ex-parte.

The delinquent employee either absents from the enquiry right from the beginning or withdraws or refuses to take part in the enquiry. In that event, the enquiry is conducted ex-parte in the absence of the delinquent employee. Evidences are taken, proceedings are made, and enquiry is concluded in the absence of the delinquent employee presuming that the delinquent is present. In ex-parte enquiry no cross-examination can be done. The enquiry officer can, however, ask any question, in the nature of clarification of doubt to fully understand the matter.

If a worker intentionally refuses to participate in the enquiry he cannot complain that the dismissal is against the principles of natural justice. *Laxmi Devi Sugar Mills v. Ram Swaroop, (1957) I LLJ 17: AIR 1957 SC 82.*

When the worker boycott the enquiry on non-fulfillment of any unreasonable demand then enquiry can proceed ex-parte. When the delinquent employee does not co-operate in enquiry on one pretext or the other then ex-parte enquiry is justified. *Brook Bond Company of India Ltd. v. Subba Raman, (1961) II LLJ 417: 20 FJR 424 (SC).*

If, however, the delinquent employee is prevented from attending the enquiry, and the enquiry is conducted *ex-parte* then it is violation of natural justice and is considered a vitiated case of domestic enquiry.

FACT

Fact means and includes anything, state of thing, or relation of things capable of being perceived by senses. Fact is any mental condition of which any person is conscious. What exists in reality and is capable of being perceived by senses and which can be registered by mental faculties is a fact.

A fact is relevant to the other fact when they are so connected that they become part of the same transaction whether they occurred at the same time and place or at different times and places. The two facts are relevant to each other when they are connected with each other in the same context.

FINE

Fine is a pecuniary punishment inflicted by the employer on the employee on certain act or omission. There may be provision in standing orders for imposition of fine. However the power to impose fine is subject to the provision of Section 8 of the Payment of Wages Act,1947.

Fine is levied after due consideration of the explanation offered in writing, or in person, contingent upon the case.

HIERARCHY OF PUNISHMENT

The theory of natural justice says that punishment must be awarded in proportion to the gravity of misconduct committed. *Culpa poena par esto* i.e., "let the punishment be proportioned to the offence".

Theoretically, for any misconduct committed by an employee his employer has the discretion to award him punishment ranging from warning letter to discharge or dismissal. It is expected that the employer would inflict punishment based on the seriousness of misconduct committed by the delinquent employee. The following punishments are inflicted as disciplinary action-

    (a) Warning
    (b) Fine
    (c) Stoppage of increment
    (d) Demotion
    (e) Suspension
    (f) Discharge or Dismissal.

For lighter nature of offence warning letter is issued for the first time. However, for repeated misconducts, and for serious nature of misconducts stern actions are taken.

INDEPENDENT PERSON

An independent person is one who is totally unconnected with a case. It is always expected that the enquiry officer will be unconnected with the case of misconduct committed by a charge-sheeted employee.

If a person who is connected with the case, or is not unknown with the case, conducts an enquiry then chances are that his subjective bias will vitiate the enquiry. It is, therefore, regarded bad in the eyes of law, and is considered a violation of the theory of natural justice.

INVESTIGATING OFFICER

An investing officer is a person appointed by the management on a complain received against any employee to investigate the charges that are made against the employee. It is duty of the investigating officer to collect facts and present them to the management whether the charges that are reported against an employee stands correct or not. Based on the report of the investigating officer a charge-sheet is framed. There may be cases when extreme confidentiality is to be maintained by the investigating officer while working on a complaint like, a theft cases , a case of bribery or corruption, or a cases of sexual harassment. If the investigating officer does not move with caution then the situation may become very volatile or it may become difficult for the investigating officer to collect facts. In Industrial enterprise a senior security or intelligence officer is generally made investigating officer to investigate the charges of theft on an employee. For employees working in government departments officers in CBI or Vigilance often conduct investigation on a complaint of corruption. The entire charge-sheet is based on the report of the investigating officer. It is wise on the part of the investigating officer to collect pictorial evidence, photographs etc. so that the charges, if they exist, stand on a sound footing. There are numerous cases in industrial enterprises when employees are victimized by keeping Company material in their vehicle or bag without their knowledge. Likewise, in complaint of sexual harassment it is duty of an investigating officer to find out that what was the approach and intention of the charged person towards the complainant, and what sort of relationship existed between the complainant and the accused before the complaint was registered. These two cases are just examples to explain the role and function of an investigating officer.

Appointment of investigating officer is made very carefully. Since the investigating officer investigates and collects records against the person against whom a complaint is registered, that person should not be made investigating officer who carries some grudge against him. Because, later at the enquiry stage the delinquent may depose that the charges have been wrongfully investigated and reported since the investigating officer had some personal grudge against him. If the delinquent employee presents some proof of any earlier bad-blood between him and the investigating officer, then even when the charges have been correctly and accurately investigated and reported, it may stand on a bad footing at the enquiry because of the element of doubt and suspicion.

On many occasions the presenting officer hands over the charge to the investigating officer to lead the management witnesses and present the case of the management on his behalf at the enquiry proceedings. In that case leading the management witnesses, cross-examination of the delinquent employee and other defence witnesses lies on the investigating officer.

LEADING QUESTION

A leading question is a question which suggests an answer which the questioner wants to hear. More often than not a leading questions requires an answer in "yes or No" terms. Enquiry Officer cannot put a leading question in the enquiry. However, enquiry officer can seek clarification on any matter from either side to understand the facts of the case.

Leading question cannot be asked to prove the guilt deliberately. It has been held by Industrial Tribunal that when the only evidence is reply to the leading question, then evidence cannot be said to be fair. *Shyamlal Gupta v. Workmen Cal. Gaz., Part I C , dt. 17.03.1966 p.195.*

MALA FIDE

Mala fide is simply 'bad faith'. Opposite of '*bona fide*' is '*mala fide*'. It is being carried out or acting in bad faith, which is not genuine, and not authentic. An action of the management which is carried out with some hidden agenda and not genuine is generally considered to be *mala fide*. When an action is challenged as being *mala fide*, it is adjudicated upon and the adjudicative action goes beyond the process and facts of the *mala fide* action and tries to unearth the real intention or motive behind the action of management which is considered as *mala fide*.

MISCONDUCT

In common parlance, improper or unlawful conduct is termed as misconduct. An exhaustive list of acts of omission and commission which constitute misconduct are generally mentioned in the Standing Orders of a Company as per Industrial Employment (Standing Orders) Act, 1946. Misconduct is always defined in the rules and regulations of any organization. Generally speaking, the acts of misconduct can be broadly grouped under the following heads:

    (a) Misconduct Relating to duty
    (b) Misconduct relating to discipline
    (c) Misconduct relating to morality

(a)Misconduct Relating to duty: Common misconducts relating to duty are –
- Not performing duty punctually
- Not performing one's assigned work
- Neglect of duty
- Absence without information, permission or leave
- Late coming for duty
- Habitual Absence
- Habitual Late Coming
- Absence from assigned place of work
- Loitering in the Company premises
- Making false attendance of Work
- Go-Slow
- Gharao
- Striking work

(b) Misconduct relating to discipline: Common misconducts relating to discipline-
- Riotous or disorderly behavior at work place
- Fighting with peers or superiors
- Using slang or filthy language

- Willful insubordination
- Insulting superiors and/or co-workers
- Vulgar language or action to sexually harass female co-worker
- Damage to property and reputation of the employer

(c) Misconduct relating to morality: Common misconducts relating to morality -
- Theft
- Fraud
- Dishonesty
- Disloyalty
- Adhering to corrupt practices
- Presentation of false data to misguide management
- Moral Turpitude

The list of 'misconduct' is not and never exhaustive. Therefore, it is generally mentioned as *"without prejudice to the general meaning of the term misconduct"*, that is to say what is believed as misconduct in the eyes of society will constitute a misconduct for which disciplinary action can be initiated against the defaulter or delinquent employee whether or not that specific misconduct has been mentioned in the list of misconduct in the Standing Orders of the Company.

Again, the grouping of the misconduct, as mentioned above, has been done for proper understanding of misconduct. In fact, they overlap.

MORAL TURPITUDE

'Moral turpitude' is composed of two words- 'moral' and 'turpitude'. 'Moral' means 'conduct or character from the point of view of right and wrong'. 'Turpitude' means 'inherent baseness or vileness'. Moral turpitude, therefore, means an act or conduct which is inherently mean, vile or bad.

The Allahabad High Court has laid down the below mentioned tests for determining whether a particular act involves moral turpitude-
(a) Whether the act leading to a conviction was such as would shock the moral conscience of society, in general
(b) Whether the motive which led to the act was a base one

(c) Whether on account of the act having been committed the perpetrator could be considered to be a depraved character of a person who was to be looked down upon by the society.

The term moral turpitude has a very wide connotation.

PERVERSE FINDING

The term perverse finding is not uncommon in connection with domestic enquiry. It depicts the biasness of the enquiry officer who acts as a vindictive agent of the management. Perverse finding is morally wrong or wicked finding of an enquiry. It is deviation from the material facts of the case. It is done with ulterior motive to victimize the charge-sheeted employee. Often, it also relates to ineptness or incompetence of the enquiry officer. The courts frown upon the perverse findings, and set aside the punishment inflicted by the employer.

There is a two-fold test to identify perversity of a finding. The first test is that, the finding is not supported by any legal evidence at all and the second test is that, on the basis of the material on record, no reasonable person could have arrived at the same findings.

PRELIMINARY ENQUIRY

A preliminary enquiry is conducted with a view to find facts whether a case is fit or not for initiating disciplinary action. Preliminary enquiry is not conducted in every case. Preliminary enquiry is a discretion of the management. In sensitive cases, where the management tries to assure that *prima facie* a case of misconduct genuinely exists, or that charges must be framed without defect, a preliminary enquiry becomes a necessity.

The investigation conducted in the course of preliminary enquiry do not form part of domestic enquiry in any way. As such, it is not obligatory to follow rules of natural justice in a preliminary enquiry.

The rules relating to domestic enquiry are not applicable in case of preliminary enquiry. In preliminary enquiry there may be *ex-parte* examination and *ex-parte* reports. The delinquent employee may also be interrogated during the preliminary enquiry. The deposition of the witnesses during investigation are merely meant to ascertain facts for judging whether *prima facie* a case for disciplinary action exists or not.

It may be mentioned that reports of the preliminary enquiry may be used against the delinquent workman at the domestic enquiry. However, the same must be substantiated and properly proved at the time of enquiry.

PRESENTING OFFICER
(MANAGEMENT REPRESENTATIVE)

Ideally, the burden of charge is to be proved by the charge-sheeting authority. But, the authority that issues charge-sheet is generally a high ranked person. To appear before the enquiry officer to present the case is often a time consuming process. It can continue for months together. Therefore, the charge-sheeting authority appoints a person, a subordinate under him, preferably from the same department, to represent the case of the management at the enquiry. This is done for administrative convenience.

The presenting officer presents the case of the management at the enquiry, leads the witnesses of the management side, and cross-examines the charge-sheeted employee and other defence witnesses. The burden of proving the charge levelled on the charge-sheeted employee lies on the management. The presenting officer exactly plays this role at the enquiry.

It may here be noted again that the enquiry officer is also appointed by the management. But, the enquiry officer is an independent and impartial person. In no case the enquiry officer should assume the role of the presenting officer.

The role of Presenting Officer will be dealt in detail in Chapter IV.

PROVED

A fact is said to be proved when after considering the matter before it, the court either believes it to exist or considers its existence so probable that a prudent man ought, under the circumstances of the particular case, to act upon the supposition, that it exists. In this context, it is also important to define what is 'Disproved' and 'Not Proved'.

Disproved: A fact is said to be disproved when after considering the matters before it, the court either believes that it does not exist, or considers it's non-existence so probable that a prudent man ought, under the circumstances of the particular case, to act upon the supposition, that it does not exist.

Not Proved: A fact is said not to be proved when it is neither proved, nor disproved.

RE-INSTATEMENT

The labour court or the tribunal has the adjudicative power to set aside an order of discharge or dismissal of an employee passed by the employer and order for his re-instatement. A re-instated employee resumes his position with back wages and/or reimbursement of all legal expenses. Re-instatement of a discharged employee is considered as a big moral defeat for the management.

SECOND SHOW CAUSE

The opportunity of second show cause in a case of domestic enquiry is given to the delinquent employee when the disciplinary authority provides the findings and conclusions of the enquiry officer along with the material evidences brought at the enquiry as well as the proceedings of the enquiry to the charge-sheeted employee and proposes that why a punishment of discharge or dismissal should not be inflicted on him for the charges levelled and subsequently proved at the enquiry. Second show cause is ordinarily given only where dismissal or discharge as punishment is contemplated.

A second show cause notice is, in fact, the accused employee's last opportunity to place his side of the case before the punishing authority who is about to take the final decision of discharge or dismissal against the accused employee based on the report of the Enquiry Officer. If the delinquent doesn't get a copy of the enquiry report he has no means of knowing what findings of the Enquiry Officer have gone against him and what have weighed with the disciplinary authority in coming to a decision as to the punishment proposed to be inflicted upon him. So whether or not rules or regulations provide for a copy of the enquiry report to be given to the accused employee, the rules of natural justice require that along with the second show cause notice the accused employee should be furnished with the same. The second show cause notice no doubt requires him only to show cause why the proposed punishment shall not be inflicted upon him. But upon perusal of his reply, the appointing authority may still take a view of his guilt.

The explanation or reply submitted by the employee is judged by the disciplinary authority on it's merit. However, an employer while finding any employee guilty of misconduct is obliged to consider the gravity of such misconduct and while awarding punishment like dismissal, the employer is also obliged to consider any extenuating circumstances like the period of service, previous record etc. This obligation is though of a directory nature, no employer is absolved from its obligation to consider the implication of such previous record while awarding punishment. After second show cause dismissal can be granted on following grounds:

- Such conduct on the part of the employee as may be deemed to be inconsistent or incompatible with the faithful discharge of his duties, or
- Such incapacity as prevents him from fulfilling his contract of service with the employer, or
- Such immorality on his part as may bring the employer in disrepute.

SUBSISTENCE ALLOWANCE

Where any workmen is suspended by the employer pending investigation or inquiry into complaints or charge of misconduct against him, the employer shall pay to such workman 'subsistence allowance'. The purpose of payment of subsistence allowance is to remove the hardship that a suspended employee may face owing to non-payment of salary during the period of suspension. The Industrial Employment (Standing Orders) Act, 1946 specifically mentions subsistence allowance to be paid to the employee under suspension at the rates mentioned below:

(a) at the rate of fifty per cent of the wages which the workman was entitled to immediately preceding the date of such suspension, for the first ninety days of suspension; and

(b) at the rate of seventy-five per cent of the such wages for the remaining period of suspension if the delay in the completion of disciplinary proceedings against such workman is not directly attributable to the conduct of such workman.

If any dispute arises regarding the subsistence allowance payable to a workman, the workman or the employer concerned may refer the dispute to the Labor Court, constituted under the Industrial Disputes Act, 1947 (14 of 1947), within the local limits of whose jurisdiction the industrial establishment wherein such workman is employed is situate and the Labor Court to which the dispute is so referred shall, after giving the parties an opportunity of being heard, decide the dispute and such decision shall be final and binding on the parties.

The rate of subsistence allowance is not always same for Industrial and non-industrial employees. It may vary depending upon the service rules relating to employees.

If an employee retires from service or superannuates while in suspension no subsistence allowance is paid to him after the date of retirement from service.

SUSPENSION

Suspension is temporary deferment of the servant and master relationship for any specific reason that is connected with indiscipline on the part of the servant. In the words of Lord Goddard, "*Suspension is dismissal mitigated at the discretion of the employer by a promise to re-employ.*" Suspension keeps the relation of master and servant in abeyance for a certain period. Suspension is of two types (a) Suspension, pending enquiry & (b) Suspension, as punishment.

(a) SUSPENSION, PENDING ENQUIRY

Suspension pending enquiry means temporary cessation of the right to work or labour or temporary deprivation of office, position or privilege. Suspension pending enquiry means suspension of the charge-sheeted person from duty till the time domestic or departmental enquiry concludes, and a decision on the findings of the enquiry officer is taken by the disciplinary authority. During the period of suspension pending enquiry the charge-sheeted employee is required to report once at the office daily, but he is kept out of duty. Since he does not work, he does not get salary but 'subsistence allowance' during the period of suspension pending enquiry.

Suspension pending enquiry is done to keep the charge-sheeted employee away from work place because the charge-sheeted employee may affect the enquiry by his presence at the work place.

If the employee is not found guilty of the charges levelled against him he resumes his duty with honour and all salary dues are also paid to him.

However, if the employee is found guilty of the charges levelled against him, then he is liable for punishment. Normally, suspension pending enquiry is done in serious charges of misconduct, and hence minimum punishment awarded is suspension as punishment. A delinquent employee may also be discharged or dismissed from service. Generally, in such an event, the effective date of discharge or dismissal is from the date of suspension pending the enquiry. It practically depends on the rules and regulations of an organization.

Suspension pending enquiry cannot be regarded as punishment for punishment presupposes the commission of an offence and till the offence is proved to the satisfaction of the management, suspension pending enquiry cannot be considered to be punishment.

(b) SUSPENSION, AS PUNISHMENT

Suspension as punishment is awarded to an employee after the charge levelled against him is proved at the enquiry. Suspension as punishment can be inflicted on a workman for a specified period under contract of service or the standing orders after the workman is found guilty of misconduct committed by him, *Ramnaresh Kumar v. State of West Bengal, (1958 ILLJ 567, 571 CAL.DB.).* The maximum duration of suspension, as punishment, is generally mentioned in the Standing Orders or Rules and Regulations of the organization.

The effect of suspension is that the relationship of the master and servant is temporarily suspended with the consequence that the servant is not bound to render the service and the master is not bound to pay. *Balvantary Ratilal Patil v. State of Maharashtra, (1968) II LLJ 700, 703 (SC).*

A suspended employee's gate pass is taken by the management, and he is not allowed to enter works. The suspended employee is not paid salary for the period of suspension.

A letter of suspension clearly mentions the dates of suspension of employee, both the start and end date inclusive in it. A copy of the suspension letter is always forwarded to the time office, wage section, establishment section, factory or works gate security.

A model suspension letter is mentioned at the end of chapter VI.

Suspension Retrospective: In the case of *Nepal Chandra Guchit v. District Magistrate, (1966, IILLJ 71 Calcutta)*, the Calcutta High Court held that suspension like other punishments like discharge or dismissal with retrospective effect is illegal and invalid. In the case of *Hemant Kumar Bhattacharya v. S.N. Mukherjee, AIR 1954, Calcutta 340 (DB)*, the Calcutta High Court held that where an order of suspension can be split into two periods of time, one retrospective and the other prospective, and the retrospective part can be severed from the prospective part, the retrospective part would be invalid and the prospective part would be perfectly valid and shall operate upon its own strength.

WARNING

Warning is a minor punishment. It must be administered in writing. In the case of *Sankar Pillai v. Kerala State, (1950 ILLJ 621 Ker.)* it was held that, warning should be administered after obtaining explanation from the workman about the act or omission alleged. The procedure to be adopted for administering warning needs not be as elaborate as that for discharge or dismissal. In the case of *Madhavan v. Commissioner of Income Tax (1983 IILLJ 356 Ker)* the question arose before the Kerala High Court, whether a departmental promotion committee can take into consideration a warning given to an employee in considering him for promotion. It was held that, a censure inflicted as a regular penalty cannot have the effect of automatically postponing the employee's promotion. It is difficult to see how a warning which is not even a punishment and which is not given in accordance with the principles of natural justice can stand on a better or stronger footing in the matter of preventing an employee's promotion.

Difference between Warning and Caution or Advisory Note: Warning is a form of punishment whereas caution or advisory note is not punishment. Accordingly, warning letter is issued after the guilt of an employee is proved in a free and fair enquiry, or after the employee has pleaded guilty of the misconduct committed by him. But, advisory note is given to prevent a person from committing any misconduct. It is given contemplating the tangent behavior, and restricting the employee from committing any misconduct.

WITHHOLDING OF INCREMENT

In the case of graded scales, increments are automatic till the stage of efficiency bar is reached. Withholding of increment before the stage of efficiency bar is reached is punishment. Such punishment can be inflicted only when a charge of inefficiency or misconduct has been proved - *Rashiklal Nandlal V. Bank of Baroda (1956 ILLJ 103 Lat.).*

UNFAIR LABOUR PRACTICE

Unfair Labour Practices are acts which are prohibited by law. Detailed list of acts comprising unfair labour practices have been mentioned in Schedule V of the Industrial Disputes Act, 1947. As is clear by the nomenclature itself the acts are considered to be unfair and hence prohibited by law. The Industrial Disputes Act mentions penalty for committing unfair labour practice. In this book the subject has been dealt in detail in Chapter VIII.

VICTIMIZATION

The word victimization has not been defined in the statute. The term victimization has been mentioned in unfair labour practices by the employer which finds a place in Schedule V of the Industrial Disputes Act, 1947. The term was considered by the Supreme Court in the case of *Bharat Bank Ltd. V. Employees reported in AIR 1950 SC 188.* The court observed: "*It (victimization) is an ordinary English word which means that a certain person has become a victim, in other words that he has been unjustly dealt with*". Supreme Court maintained that the word 'victimization', is being the victim of 'arbitrary and unfair action' of the employer.

If an employer takes arbitrary disciplinary action against an employee it is called 'victimization'. The victimization of an employee can be done by the employer for any reason whatsoever, which is not genuine and legitimate, and contains ulterior motive. It is aimed at putting the employee to unreasonable suffering. The most important reason for victimization is considered as trade union activities of the employee. However, there can be any other reason typical to a case of victimization.

If an employee is punished by employer when he is innocent, or is awarded punishment out of proportion for any misconduct committed by him, it becomes a case of victimization. In fact, victimization is a multi-headed monster which is tackled by industrial adjudication.

Even when the services are terminated in accordance with the Standing Orders, the Tribunal can enquire into the causes, to find out whether it was a bona fide exercise of power, or was a colourable exercise of power or was the result of victimization or unfair labour practice. *Hajee Ismail Said & Sons (P) Ltd. v. Fourth Industrial Tribunal, AIR 1966 Cal 375: (1966) II LLJ 59.*

WITNESS

One who gives evidence in a cause before a court of law or quasi-judicial enquiry is called a witness. A witness has the knowledge of the act of misconduct or case and comes at the enquiry to depose the fact or incident. A witness in broad sense is one who attests to matter of fact in course of a judicial process. Both, the prosecution and the defence side present their own witness at the enquiry. A witness is subject to cross-examination by the other side.

WITNESS TURNING HOSTILE OR HOSTILE WITNESS

A hostile witness is like a player who tries to shoot goal in his own side. A witness is termed as hostile when he speaks in favour of the opposite side, and tries to hold his own side at fault. A hostile witness is, therefore, cross-examined not by the other side but by the side which produces the witness at the enquiry.

CHAPTER IV

ROLE OF ENQUIRY OFFICER, PRESENTING OFFICER & PUNISHING AUTHORITY

It is imperative to separately mention the roles of enquiry officer, presenting officer and the punishing authority for a clear understanding of the roles and responsibilities of the three important functionaries in a domestic or departmental enquiry.

THE ROLE OF ENQUIRY OFFICER

The enquiry officer is the pivotal point around which the entire enquiry rotates. It is the enquiry officer who actually conducts the enquiry, and verifies whether the charges made against an employee are correct or not. As such, an enquiry officer plays the role of a judge in recoding witnesses and examining evidences. Based on the material facts present at the enquiry he takes a decision whether the charges levelled against the employee stands fully proved, partially proved or not proved at all.

An Enquiry Officer is appointed by the Disciplinary Authority. The same Disciplinary Authority who inflicts charges of misconduct on the delinquent employee, also appoints a Presenting Officer to prove the charges inflicted on the delinquent employee. Therefore, the enquiry officer is always looked upon with suspicion by the charged employee. It requires tremendous amount of goodwill and impartiality on the part of an enquiry officer to win the confidence of both the charged employee and the management to successfully discharge his role of an impartial judge in the enquiry.

Therefore, the selection and appointment of an enquiry officer is always very important task in the hands of the disciplinary authority.

APPOINTMENT OF AN ENQUIRY OFFICER :

The appointment of an enquiry officer is made by the disciplinary authority to find out the veracity of the allegation or the charge of misconduct levelled on an employee of the organization. The competent authority to appoint an enquiry officer in an organization is the authority on whom the power to award punishment is entrusted. It may be simply understood that the appointing authority has the power to punish and remove an employee. But, because of the vastness of the organization sometimes the disciplinary powers are delegated at the appropriate levels in the organizations. Only a competent authority can issue a charge-sheet on receipt of a complaint against an employee, and appoint an enquiry officer to enquire into the charges against the delinquent employee.

The rules regarding the appointment of an enquiry officer are ordinarily mentioned in the disciplinary procedure. For example, Rule 9 (2) of the Railway Servants (Discipline & Appeal) Rules, 1968 refers to the appointment of Inquiry Officer (IO). It provides that " whenever the Disciplinary Authority (DA) is of the opinion that there are grounds for inquiring into the truth of any imputation or misconduct or misbehaviour of a railway servant, it may itself inquire into the truth thereof or appoint an authority to inquire into the truth thereof." However, unless it is unavoidable, the disciplinary authority should refrain from being the Inquiry Officer and should instead appoint another officer for the purpose of conducting inquiry.

WHO SHOULD BE APPOINTED AS INQUIRY OFFICER :

The person to be appointed as the enquiry officer should fulfill the following requisites :
- He Should not be interested in the subject matter of the inquiry in any manner;
- He should not be biased;
- He should not be a witness in the proceedings;
- He should not have expressed an opinion about the merits of the case;
- He should be sufficiently senior to evoke confidence of all concerned;

THE DELINQUENT EMPLOYEE MAY ALLEGE BAISNESS AGAINST AN ENQUIRY OFFICER :

A charged employee cannot be put into any disadvantageous position in any enquiry proceeding , otherwise it can vitiate the enquiry. Therefore, a charge-sheeted employee has the right to complaint about the biasness of the enquiry officer, by assigning proper reasons thereof, at any stage of the enquiry. Such a complaint is addressed to the management or the authority which has appointed the enquiry officer. Whenever an application alleging bias against the Enquiry Officer is moved by the Charged employee, the proceedings should be stayed and the authority should take appropriate decision in this regard. The authority can either remove the enquiry officer and appoint a new enquiry officer in his place, if the allegation of the charged employee of biasness of the enquiry officer is found to be correct. The authority may, however, decline the request of the charged employee to remove the enquiry officer if the charge of biasness is found to be frivolous and perky.

CHANGE OF ENQUIRY OFFICER:

An Enquiry Officer may be changed during the course of an enquiry. If an enquiry officer is changed in the middle of an inquiry, the new Enquiry Officer shall hear the case from the stage which it had already reached. Before beginning the proceedings of the enquiry the new enquiry officer must make it sure that the charged employee does not have any reservations about the past proceedings of the enquiry, and the concurrence of the employee should be recorded in the proceedings. In case, the charged employee expresses any doubt about any specific part of the proceedings, and he states the same with plausible reasons, then the new Enquiry Officer must act in a manner which leaves no apprehensions on the part of the charged employee.

FUNCTIONS OF ENQUIRY OFFICER :

Though the Enquiry Officer is appointed by the disciplinary authority, he is not subject to the directions or influence of the latter in regard to the conduct of enquiry, evaluation of evidence, or his findings. If the Disciplinary Authority or the Punishing Authority interferes in enquiry, and the Enquiry Officer is influenced by them, then the enquiry gets vitiated. *Mahadayal Premchandra v. Commercial Tax Officer, AIR 1958 SC 667: 1959 SCR 551.*

An Enquiry Officer is expected to function independently without any interference in the discharge of his functions. To enable the Enquiry Officer to hold the inquiry, the Disciplinary Authority or the Punishing Authority is required to furnish copies of the following documents to the Inquiry Officer along with his letter of appointment, or immediately thereafter.

- A copy of the articles of charge and the statement of imputations of misconduct or misbehavior along with the list of documents on the basis of which the charges have been made.
- Copies of the statements of witnesses, if any, recorded during the preliminary inquiry/investigation by which the articles of charge are proposed to be sustained.
- Evidence proving the delivery of the relevant documents to the charged employee;
- A copy of the statement of defence, if any, submitted by the charged employee or a clear statement that the charged employee has not replied to the charge sheet within the specified time; and
- Orders appointing the Presentation Officer who will present the prosecution charge at the enquiry and lead the prosecution witnesses.

On receipt of the above documents, the enquiry officer after studying the documents, send a notice to the charged employee intimating him the place, time and date of enquiry if the charge-sheet itself does not contain an information in this regard. The enquiry Officer must make it sure that proper time and opportunity has been provided to the accused employee to prepare his defences. Providing too little time i.e., of two days only may not be sufficient to start enquiry. *Unnati Mills, Amritsar v. Workmen Punj. Govt. Gazette dt. 25.11.1960 Part I, p. 2901.*

RECORDING AND MAINTAINING DAILY ORDER SHEET:

Immediately on receipt of his order of appointment, the Enquiry Officer should open a "Daily Order Sheet". Daily Order Sheet thus contains a running record of all important events occurring during the course of the enquiry as well as the record of the business transacted on each day of the hearing and the orders passed by the Enquiry Officer on oral or written representation of both the parties, i.e. Presenting Officer and the charged employee.

It was mentioned in the case of *A. K. Das v. Sr. Suptd. Of Post Office, AIR 1969 A & N 99,* that in the absence of an order sheet, it is difficult to know whether at the various stages, the Enquiry Officer has violated the procedure without prejudicing any of the rights of the Government servant.

The entries in the daily order sheet should be signed by the Enquiry Officer to authenticate them. The entries relating to each date of hearing should also be signed by the Presenting Officer and the charged employee with date. Since the daily order sheet is a record of important happenings during the course of enquiry maintained by the Enquiry Officer, it has to be as per his direction. If the charged employee refuses to sign or records an objection on the order sheet at the time of signing, the enquiry officer should record the fact of refusal to sign by the charged employee and further give his comments on the objection and sign the record. He should not enter into an argument with the charged employee on this account. This is because the Supreme Court in the case of *Union of India v. T. R. Verma, AIR 1957 SC 882,* has held that in the event of a dispute arising as to what happened before the Inquiry Tribunal, the statement of the Presiding Officer (Enquiry Officer) in that regard is generally to be taken as correct. The daily order sheet should generally contain:

(i)   Date-wise brief record of all important happenings in the course of enquiry;
(ii)Brief statement of all oral or written representations by the charged employee or the Presenting Officer and orders passed thereon by the Enquiry Officer;
(iii) Record of business transacted on each day of oral hearing, and
(iv) Orders of the Enquiring Authority for holding of hearings, their adjournments, etc.

ENQUIRY OFFICER SHOULD ENSURE RELEVANT WITNESSES

It is the duty of the enquiry officer to ensure relevant witnesses at the enquiry. The enquiry officer can demand a list of witnesses from the prosecution and defence side and ascertain as to what important matter connecting to the charge they would depose at the enquiry. If the list of witnesses is very long, and the witnesses are not going to depose any material fact, and will be only repetitive, then the enquiry officer can ask to curtail names from the list of witnesses so provided. However, the enquiry officer must act with caution in this regard.

If the Enquiry Officer refuses to allow any defence witness at the enquiry then he must state the reasons thereof. *A. R. S. Choudhary v. Union of India, (1957) I LLJ 494 Cal. H.C.*

It is duty of the enquiry officer to assist the delinquent employee in producing his witness. The enquiry officer should formally request the management to release any particular employee to give witness at the enquiry. However, primarily it is the duty of the charge-sheeted employee to manage his own witness.

ENQUIRY OFFICER SHOULD REMAIN IMPARTIAL THROUGHOUT THE PROCEEDINGS

The Enquiry Officer should remain impartial during the enquiry proceedings. He must follow the rules of natural justice all throughout in dispensing the case. He should not form any opinion till recording the last evidence in the case. He should reach at a logical finding only after properly weighing the evidences and materials on record. The principles of natural justice demand that the officer making enquiry should not be interested in proving the charged employee guilty at any cost. *A.R.S. Choudhary v. Union of India AIR 1956 Cal 662.*

ENQUIRY OFFICER SHOULD NOT ASSUME ROLE OF PRESENTING OFFICER: HE SHOULD NOT CROSS-EXAMINE

At no point of time during the procedure of enquiry, the enquiry officer should try to assume the role of a presenting officer. He should not cross-examine any witness in the enquiry. But, for seeking explanation of any connected matter or to clarify any point, the enquiry officer can ask non probing questions.

ENQUIRY OFFICER CANNOT ADD NEW CHARGE OR AMEND THE CHARGE-SHEET

The enquiry officer is an appointee of the disciplinary authority or the punishing authority. He conducts enquiry on delegated powers by the disciplinary authority or the punishing authority and the power to frame charges rests with the latter. As such, the enquiry officer cannot amend the charge-sheet or add any new charge. If the enquiry officer discovers any anomaly in the charge-sheet then he should bring this to the notice of the disciplinary authority or punishing authority and get the same amended promptly.

ENQUIRY OFFICER SHOULD NOT ASK LEADING QUESTIONS

The enquiry Officer should not ask leading questions in the enquiry either to the charge-sheeted employee or his witness.

If a leading question purports to holding someone guilty, or even providing a hint in that respect, then it would vitiate the enquiry. It has been held by the Tribunal that when the only evidence is reply to the leading question then evidence cannot be said to be fair. *Firestone Tyre and Rubber Co. Ltd. v. Workmen, (1967)2 LLJ 715 (SC): AIR 1968 SC 236.*

The Enquiry Officer, however, can ask questions for clarification of any matter relating to the enquiry.

STANDARD OF PROOF:

A departmental enquiry is inherently different from judicial proceedings in a Court of Law and need not be carried out rigidly in accordance with the rules applicable to judicial proceedings. The enquiry officer must weigh the evidences very carefully to determine the standard of proof. The Supreme Court has held that standard of proof required in a disciplinary case is that of '**preponderance of probability**' and not '**proof beyond reasonable doubt**'.

Preponderance of evidence is contrast to beyond reasonable doubt which is more severe test of evidence required to convict in a criminal case. It is greater weight of the evidence required in a case to decide in favour of one side or the other. This preponderance is based on the more convincing evidence and its probable truth or accuracy.

The enquiry Officer should ensure that reasonable opportunity is given to the accused for defending himself in the course of inquiry and weigh the evidences on the basis of probable truth of the charge as indicated by the materials on record.

As 'beyond all reasonable doubt' evidence is not applicable in departmental enquiry, the enquiry officer cannot decide a case on 'benefit of doubt' basis.

REPORT BY THE ENQUIRY OFFICER:

After the evidence has been taken and the arguments are over, the enquiry officer writes his report. The enquiry officer should prepare a report on each of the charges, supported by reasons thereof. He should indicate whether the charge(s) is/are fully established, partially established or not established. The scope of the enquiry should be strictly limited to the charges as mentioned in the charge-sheet and which are not admitted by the accused. The enquiry officer's report should be concise and confined to the subject of the charges. In the enquiry report, the actual findings should be in respect of each of the charges indicated in the charge-sheet and enquired into, and the wording of the findings on each of the charges should be clear, precise and unequivocal and not couched in vague phraseology.

When the report of the enquiry officer is very short which does not mention the names of the witnesses or the nature of evidences produced and does not give any reason for holding that the charges were confirmed, then that report vitiates the enquiry. *M.P. State Road Transport Corporation v. Industrial Tribunal (1971) 40 FLR 448 (M.P. HC).*

Other facts coming to the notice of the enquiry officer during the course of enquiry which have no direct bearing on the charges but cannot be neglected can be recorded in a separate note, but should not form part of the enquiry report. The enquiry officer should not mention any extraneous matter in the enquiry report and should not base his findings on any such extraneous matter. The findings of the enquiry officer must relate to materials on record. Otherwise, the principles of natural justice is vitiated.

The report of the enquiry Officer must relate to the charges only. It should not be arbitrary. *Harbans Singh v. State of Punjab, AIR 1962 Punj. 289.*

The Enquiry Officer must record the findings with reasons for the same, because unless this is done there can be no surety that the decision is based on proper evidence. *Sur Enamel and Stamping Works v. Workmen, (1963) 2 LLJ 376: AIR 1963 SC 1914.*

In the case of *Anandram Jiandra Vaswani v. Union of India,1983 (2) LLN 510:1983 Lab IC 624, Cal. H.C.,* the High Court has held that it can interfere in the findings of enquiry in the following circumstances-

■ The enquiry officer has arrived at a finding based on no evidence.
■ The findings are inconsistent with the evidence or contradictory to it.
■ The enquiry officer has acted on material partly relevant and partly irrelevant.
■ The enquiry officer has drawn upon his own imagination and imported facts and circumstances not apparent from the record.
■ The enquiry officer has based his own conclusion on mere conjectures and surmises.

- No reasonable person could have come to findings as has been arrived at by the enquiry officer.
- The enquiry officer has ignored the material evidence and has cast the onus of proof upon the accused person.

An enquiry officer must put the above mentioned points while writing an enquiry report.

ENQUIRY OFFICER SHOULD NOT PRESCRIBE PUNISHMENT

The enquiry officer should not prescribe any punishment. It is basically outside the scope of work for the enquiry officer because an enquiry officer conducts enquiry at the delegated powers of the disciplinary authority or punishing authority and his sole work is to find out the veracity of the charges as mentioned in the charge-sheet.

SUBMISSION OF THE REPORT TO THE DISCIPLINARY AUTHORITY

The enquiry officer should submit the complete report of enquiry to the disciplinary authority. The enquiry officer becomes *functus officio* after he has submitted his report to the disciplinary authority. A copy of the enquiry Report eventually is required to be furnished to the accused employee.

STAY OF PROCEEDINGS:

The enquiry officer should not normally stay the proceedings of an enquiry except under orders of a Court or under written orders of disciplinary authority who should record detailed reasons for such orders.

IMPORTANT DO'S AND DON'T'S FOR THE ENQUIRY OFFICER:

DO'S

- Keep an impartial and humanitarian approach as enquiry officer.
- Explain the process of enquiry to the delinquent employee, and his co-worker, if allowed at the enquiry.
- Be well conversant with the rules and regulations of the organization.
- Have thorough knowledge of rules of natural justice and disciplinary procedure of the organization.

- Note down the proceedings at the enquiry very meticulously.
- Put questions for clarification of any point.
- Complete enquiry without any inordinate delay.
- Make report of enquiry based on evidences and materials presented at the enquiry.

DON'T'S

- Do not consider it a management duty to assist the presenting officer in proving the charge.
- Do not assume the role of Presenting Officer or Management representative at any time during the process of enquiry.
- Do not carry any bias against the delinquent employee.
- Do not ask leading questions in the enquiry.
- Do not note down any point in the enquiry proceedings without full understanding of the same.
- Do not allow any irrelevant witness.
- Do not allow the delinquent to adopt dilatory tactics.
- Do not hold an employee guilty on suspicion or surmise.
- Do not base findings of the enquiry on personal knowledge or extraneous matters
- Do not prescribe punishment.

THE ROLE OF PRESENTING OFFICER OR MANAGEMENT REPRESENTATIVE:

The presenting officer or the management representative plays a very important role in the enquiry. His role is similar to the role of a public prosecutor. He is the representative of management to prove the charges imposed on the delinquent employee. He presents the case of the management at the enquiry, leads prosecution witnesses and cross-examines the delinquent employee and defence witnesses. The burden of proving the charge, in a sense, rests on the presenting officer or the management representative. A presenting officer, therefore, has to be a good communicator, a good listener, a logical thinker, well versed with the rules and regulations of the organization and very effective in the art of cross-examination of witnesses. A presenting officer or a management representative has to be very assertive.

The selection and appointment of a Presenting Officer is, therefore, always very important task in the hands of the disciplinary authority.

APPOINTMENT OF PRESENTING OFFICER :

The appointment of presenting officer or management representative is made by the punishing authority or the disciplinary authority. Generally, the competent authority that appoints an enquiry officer also appoints a presenting officer. The rules regarding the appointment of a presenting officer is normally mentioned in the disciplinary procedure of the organization. A management representative or the presenting officer is generally a senior employee of the same department to which the delinquent or the charged employee belongs. It is because he is well versed with the working of the department and knows the technicalities involved in the case.

At the time of appointment of the management representative the disciplinary or the charge-sheet issuing authority hands over copy of the charge-sheet, preliminary report of investigation on which charges were framed, reply of the delinquent in response to the charge-sheet, list of witnesses and other documents related with the case.

The delinquent or the charged employee needs to be informed about the presenting officer who would be leading the case of the management against him at the enquiry proceedings, and letter of authorization issued by the Punishing Authority in this regard also needs to be exhibited. This is done at the beginning of the enquiry proceedings.

RESPONSIBILITIES OF THE PRESENTING OFFICER :

- The presenting officer prepares the case of the management and presents it at the enquiry.
- He prepares the witnesses of the management to be produced at the enquiry. Preparation here means preparing questionnaire about the possible questions that may be asked by the defence side at the time of cross-examination.
- He cross- examines the statement of the delinquent employee, as also the witnesses produced by the defence side.
- He opposes the dilatory tactics of the defence side aimed to unnecessarily prolong the enquiry proceedings.
- He makes available the documents which are required from the management at the enquiry.

CHANGE OF PRESENTING OFFICER OR HANDING OVER CHARGE TO INVESTIGATING OFFICER:

Presenting Officer is ordinarily not changed by the management because it is not considered good for the management to change its own prosecution leader. However, it is perfectly alright for the management representative to hand over the charge to the investigating officer, if any, to act on his behalf at the enquiry. It is because, in some cases like theft case, embezzlement of fund etc. the Chief Vigilance Officer or the Security Officer who is the investigating officer carries detailed knowledge of the investigation of the concerned case, and the main witnesses are also from the same department. Therefore, to further lead the case and present witnesses on behalf of the management it becomes easier for the investigating officer. Once the presenting officer hands over the charge to the investigating officer, the examination of witnesses from management side and cross-examination of the charged employee, and the witnesses from the defence side becomes the responsibility of the investigating officer.

IMPORTANT DO'S & DON'T'S FOR PRESENTING OFFICER:

DO'S :

- Study all the documents based on which the charges have been framed and try to make a mental framework of how the prosecution would proceed at the enquiry.
- Carefully read the explanation submitted by the charged employee, and try to read between the lines.
- Take down notes of important facts. Prepare the statements to be made at the enquiry.
- Collect and keep ready all the documents to be submitted at the enquiry.
- Before presentation of a prosecution witness at the enquiry prepare him well with the case and equip him well for the cross examination.
- Try to anticipate the points that the charged employee or the defence witnesses would raise at the enquiry, and prepare appropriate answers to them.
- Be thorough with the rules and regulations of the organization, as also with the disciplinary procedure of the organization.

Assist the enquiry officer to avoid any procedural mistake in the enquiry.

■ Present fresh witnesses at the enquiry to clarify some points related with the case. The right opportunity is when all other prosecution witnesses have been exhausted, and before the defence side presents the case.

DON'T'S:

■ Do not try to show friendliness with the enquiry officer.
■ Do not get adjournment where it can be avoided.
■ Do not procrastinate in submission of statements or other documents to the enquiry officer when required.
■ Do not examine witnesses on issues not relevant with the charge to be proved.
■ Do not take any prosecution witness directly at the enquiry without discussing the matter to be deposed.

THE ROLE OF PUNISHING AUTHORITY OR DISCIPLINARY AUTHORITY:

DESCRIPION OF PUNISHING AUTHORITY:

The punishing or disciplinary authority in an organization is competent to punish an employee for his act of misconduct. Basically, the employer, who appoints an employee has the power to punish the employee. The punishment can range from a minor punishment to a major punishment like dismissal from the service of the employer. As in big organizations all the employees do not have interface with the employer or directors of the Company, the powers of appointment and taking disciplinary action against an employee is generally delegated to appropriate levels in the organization. Based on this delegation of authority the appropriate competent authority is empowered to take disciplinary action against an employee. Since the punishing authority delegates his powers in case of disciplinary actions, it is always open for any disciplinary or punishing authority to himself conduct domestic enquiry.

A PUNISHING AUTHORITY CAN HIMSELF CONDUCT ENQUIRY

An enquiry officer conducts an enquiry on the basis of delegated powers by the punishing authority. Hence, a punishing authority can himself also conduct an enquiry, and also decide about the punishment to be awarded to the delinquent employee in case the charge is established in the enquiry.

PUNISHING AUTHORITY MAY NOT AGREE WITH THE ENQUIRY OFFICER

The punishing authority may not agree with the enquiry officer. The punishing authority must apply its mind while awarding punishment. When the punishing authority agrees with the findings of the enquiry officer then he need not give any reason for awarding a punishment. However, when the punishing authority does not agree with the findings of the enquiry officer, based on the material on record, he is required to give reasons for the punishment awarded by him. *A.R.S. Choudhary v. Union Of India, 1957 I LLJ 494 (Cal H.C).; State of Assam v. Bimal Kumar, AIR 1963, SC 1612; Narayan Misra v. State of Orissa, (1969) SLR 657 (SC).*

SECOND SHOW CAUSE CAN BE ISSUED BY PUNISHING AUTHORITY ONLY

A second show cause notice can be issued by either punishing authority or a disciplinary authority to whom the power to inflict punishment has been delegated by the punishing authority in writing. A second show cause notice is issued immediately before awarding the final punishment to a delinquent employee whose guilt has been proved in an enquiry. The purpose of the second show cause notice is two fold. First, to award an opportunity to the delinquent employee to represent against a proposed harsh punishment like, dismissal from service. And second, to provide an opportunity to the delinquent employee to acquaint himself with the findings of the enquiry officer. Otherwise, the delinquent employee will have no opportunity to challenge the findings of the enquiry officer before the punishment is inflicted on him. It is because, the enquiry officer gives his report only, and directly, to the disciplinary or punishing authority who has to take a decision regarding the punishment.

It has been held in the case of *Firestone Tyre and Rubber Company v. Workmen (AIR 1968 SC 236)*, that failure to give copies of the minutes of the enquiry before asking him to reply to the second show cause notice did not vitiate the enquiry because the minutes were recorded in the presence of the workman. A second Show cause notice must , therefore, contain the report of the enquiry officer and other important connecting papers, if not the entire minutes of the enquiry.

In case of *Ramdulary v. Union of India, 1973, Lab IC 136 (All HC),* it was observed that when the Chief Engineer was the appointing authority then the Divisional Engineer could not possess the powers of a punishing authority, and a second show cause issued by Divisional Engineer was not correct course of disciplinary action. The contention is that it is the disciplinary authority, invested with the powers of a punishing authority, who considers the explanation and gives punishment. *The same contention has been held in Shardul Singh v. State of M.P. AIR 1966 M.P.193; K. K. Murti v. South Eastern Railway AIR, 1958, Cal. 633.*

The points raised by the delinquent employee in response to the second show cause must be considered by the punishing authority.

PUNISHING AUTHORITY CAN CONSIDER PAST RECORD OF EMPLOYEE

Punishing Authority can consider past record of the employee before awarding punishment. The consideration of past record is mandatory, if the rules and regulations so require. Otherwise, it is optional. If the past record of the employee is considered by the Punishing Authority while awarding punishment, the delinquent employee should be properly informed in this regard. The delinquent employee must have the full knowledge, and opportunity for representation when past record is considered to exacerbate the punishment.

PUNISHING AUTHORITY CAN ORDER FRESH ENQUIRY ON THE SAME CHARGES

The punishing authority can issue orders for a fresh enquiry on the same charges.

When the order of dismissal passed by the punishing authority is quashed by the Court on technical or procedural point, and not on the merits of the case, then the punishing authority can order second enquiry on the same charges. *Gopinathan Nair v. State of Kerala, (1960) I LLJ 311: AIR 1960 Ker 63).*

POWER TO INFLICT PUNIHMENT:

Only a competent authority has the right to punish an employee in the organization. That authority only has the right to punish who has the powers to issue a show-cause or a charge-sheet to an employee. An authority above that level also has the powers to inflict punishment, but no authority below that has any authority to punish.

While awarding punishment the punishing authority must follow the general norms regarding punishment. These are –

(a) No punishment should be awarded which is not mentioned in the rules and regulation or Standing Orders of the Company.

(b) No punishment should be awarded which is disproportionate to the Offence.

(c) No punishment should be awarded which is discretionary, and discriminates one employee from the other.

(d) No punishment should be awarded for a charge not mentioned in the charge-sheet, or not established in the enquiry.

IMPORTANT DO'S AND DON'T'S FOR THE PUNISHING AUTHORITY:

DO'S

- Appoint an impartial Enquiry Officer and an efficient Presenting Officer.
- Disconnect from the day-to day enquiry proceedings.
- Conduct enquiry, if required, as an enquiry officer.
- Consider the report of enquiry in critical manner and decide whether to agree fully or partially with the findings of the enquiry officer, or to disagree totally and order for a fresh enquiry.
- Record own findings, if disagreeing with the report of the enquiry officer.
- In case of multiple charges on a delinquent employee consider each charge separately.
- Give reasons for punishment.
- Give a second show cause notice to the charged employee if the delinquent deserves a severe punishment.
- Provide copy of the enquiry report along with the second show cause notice.
- Consideration of the past record of the employee, if required, while deciding punishment.

DON'T'S:

- Do not impose double punishment on the employee.
- Do not impose a punishment not mentioned in the service rules or standing orders of the organization.
- Do not impose discriminatory punishment for same or similar nature of offence.
- Do not make inordinate delay in awarding punishment.

CHAPTER V

EVIDENCES & WITNESSES IN
DOMESTIC ENQUIRY

The Evidence Act, strictly speaking, is not applicable in domestic enquiries. The enquiry officer in domestic enquiry is not bound to follow the provisions of the Indian Evidence Act. He cannot summon witnesses like a Court of law. He is not also expected to examine witnesses under oath as per the provisions of Oaths Act. The duty of the enquiry officer is to allow witnesses at the enquiry from the prosecution as well as the defence side, and take evidences to arrive at a reasonable conclusion whether the charge levelled on the delinquent stands proved or not. Nonetheless, the enquiry officer has to rely for his findings on the evidences and witnesses produced at the enquiry. Therefore, fundamental knowledge of evidences and witnesses and basic acumen to weigh them on the basis of their importance is desirable on the part of the enquiry officer.

WHAT IS AN EVIDENCE

The word 'Evidence' has been derived from the Latin word 'evidere' which implies 'to show distinctly', 'to make clear to view or sight', 'to discover clearly', 'to make certain', 'to prove' etc. Evidence means through argument to prove or disprove any matter of fact the truth of which is submitted to judicial investigation. Evidence signifies that which demonstrates, makes clear or ascertain the truth of the facts or points in favour of one side or the other.

Evidence includes everything that is used to determine or demonstrate the truth of an assertion. Procurement of evidence is the process of using those things that are either presumed to be true, or which are proved by evidence, to demonstrate the truth of an assertion. Evidence helps in establishing the burden of proof.

WHAT IS MEANT BY WITNESS

A witness is a person who has the knowledge of fact or incident and comes at the enquiry to depose the fact or incident. Witness in a case is presented by both the prosecution side as well as the defence side.

Prosecution Witness

Prosecution is the institution or commencement of criminal proceeding and the process of exhibiting formal charges against an offender before a legal or quasi-legal authority, and pursuing them to final judgment on behalf of authority that implicate the charge. A prosecution exists until a decision on charge is not pronounced by the judging authority, whether acquittal or conviction. A witness which appears on behalf of the prosecution side is known as a Prosecution Witness.

Defence Witness

Defence side opposes or denies the truth or validity of the prosecutor's complaint. In the proceedings, the defendant or the accused party or his legal agents deny the charge and defend the accused. A witness appearing from defending party is known as a Defence Witness.

AN EVIDENCE OR A WITNESS NEEDS TO BE CROSS-EXAMINED TO BECOME VALID

It is important to note that if the decision making authority relies on any particular evidence or witness, that evidence or witness must have been cross-examined. Otherwise, it cannot be relied upon in deciding a case. An evidence or a witness, to be valid and legal, must pass the test of cross-examination.

On many occasions, the cases decided by the enquiry officers are held defective by the court of law because of this single anomaly in the domestic enquiry.

PRESENTATION OF EVIDENCES AND WITNESSES

In law, the production and presentation of evidence depends first on establishing on whom the burden of proof lays. Two primary burden-of-proof considerations exist in law. The first is on whom the burden rests. In general, the burden of proof is placed on the prosecution. The person bringing the charge has to prove the charge. The second consideration is the degree of certitude or sureness proof must reach, depending on both the quantity and quality of evidence. These degrees are different for criminal and civil cases, the former requiring evidence beyond reasonable, the latter considering only which side has the preponderance of evidence, or whether the proposition is more likely true or false. The decision maker or the judge, decides whether the burden of proof has been fulfilled, or not. Firstly, it is decided who will carry the burden of proof, then evidence are gathered and presented to decide the case.

CLASSIFICATION OF EVIDENCE

Oral and Documentary, are two broad classification of evidence. There are other classifications used in relation to evidence. It is desirable to understand them all, and the value they attach in deciding any particular case.

Oral Evidence

The statements which a decision making authority or judge permits or requires to be made before it by witnesses, in relation to matters of fact under enquiry are called oral evidence.

Section 60 of the Indian Evidence Act, 1872 prescribed the provision of recording oral evidence. All those statements which the court permits or expects the witnesses to make in his presence regarding the truth of the facts are called Oral Evidence. Oral Evidence is that evidence which the witness has personally seen or heard. Oral evidence must always be direct or positive. Evidence is direct when it goes straight to establish the main fact in issue.

Documentary Evidence

The documents, including electronic records, produced for the inspection by a decision making authority or judge are called documentary evidence. Section 3 of The Indian Evidence Act says that all those documents which are presented in the court for inspection such documents are called documentary evidences.

Primary Evidence & Secondary Evidence
Primary Evidence

The Indian Evidence Act in section 62 mentions primary evidence as the top-most class of evidences. It is that proof which in any possible condition gives the vital hint in a disputed fact and establishes through documentary evidence on the production of an original document for inspection by the court. It means the original document itself produced for the inspection of the court. In Lucas v. Williams the Privy Council held "Primary Evidence is evidence which the law requires to be given first, and secondary evidence is the evidence which may be given in the absence of that better evidence when a proper explanation of its absence has been given."

Secondary Evidence

The Indian Evidence Act in Section 63 says Secondary Evidence is the inferior evidence. It is evidence that occupies a secondary position. It is such evidence on the presentation of which it is felt that superior evidence yet remains to be produced. It is the evidence which is produced in the absence of the primary evidence therefore it is known as secondary evidence.

If in place of primary evidence secondary evidence is admitted without any objection at the proper time then the parties are precluded from raising the question that the document has not been proved by primary evidence but by secondary evidence. But where there is no secondary evidence as contemplated by Section 66 of the Evidence Act then the document cannot be said to have been proved either by primary evidence or by secondary evidence."

It may be concluded, thus, that proof rests on a primary evidence that is directly related to the case. In absence of primary evidence a secondary evidence is required to prove a point. In the absence of both a point will be not be taken to be proved.

Real Evidence & Personal Evidence:

Real Evidence

Real Evidence means real or material evidence. Real evidence of a fact is brought to the knowledge before a judge or decision making authority by inspection of a physical object and not by information derived from a witness or a document.

Personal evidence

Personal Evidence is that evidence which is afforded by human agents, either by way of disclosure or by voluntary sign before the decision making authority or the judge.

Direct Evidence & Indirect Evidence

Direct Evidence

Direct Evidence is that evidence which is very important for the decision of the matter in issue. The main facts of the case, or the issues involved in a case when they are presented by witnesses who have themselves seen them, or the main documentary proof which are original and authentic and have direct bearing on the matter is said to be direct evidence.

Indirect Evidence or Circumstantial Evidence

There is no distinction between indirect evidence and circumstantial evidence . Circumstantial Evidence attempts to prove the facts in issue by providing other facts and affords an instance as to its existence. It is that which relates to a series of other facts than the fact in issue but by experience have been found so associated with the fact in issue in relation of cause and effect that it leads to a satisfactory conclusion.

In *Hanumant Govind Narundkar v. State of Madhya Pradesh (AIR 1952, SC 343)* , The Hon'ble *Supreme Court* Observed, "In dealing with circumstantial evidence there is always the danger that suspicion may take the place of legal proof. It is well to remember that in cases where the evidence is of a circumstantial nature the circumstances from which the conclusion of guilt is to be drawn should in the first instance, be fully established and all the facts so established should be consistent only with the hypothesis of the guilt of the accused. In other words there can be a chain of evidence so far complete as not to leave any reasonable ground for a conclusion consistent with the innocence of the accused and it must be such as to show that within all human probability the act must have been done by the accused."

In the case of *Ashok Kumar v. State of Madhya Pradesh*, the Hon'ble *Supreme Court* has held that -

(1) The circumstances from which an inference of guilt is sought to be drawn must be cogently and firmly established.

(2) Those circumstances should be of a definite tendency unerringly pointing towards the guilt of accused.

(3) The circumstances, taken cumulatively should from a chain so complete that there is no escape from the conclusion that within all human probability the crime was committed by the accused and none else.

(4) The Circumstantial Evidence in order to sustain conviction must be complete and incapable of explanation on any other hypothesis than that of the guilt of the accused and such evidence should not only be consistent with the guilt of the accused but should be inconsistent with his innocence.

The question that which evidence is superior is going from a long time. Legal experts hold different views. Some legal experts hold the view direct evidence is superior evidence. When a particular witness says that he had seen a particular event happening then undoubtedly his evidence is superior. But, relying on direct evidence without any snag is risky because a witness can make a completely false statement. In the same manner in the case of circumstantial evidence circumstances are also proved by witnesses. Particularly the manner in which the court draws inferences from circumstances they can be wrong also, and thus circumstances also become false. However, as a rule direct evidence is given more importance in comparison to indirect or circumstantial evidence.

To understand circumstantial evidence a criminal suit of Kallu v. State Of Uttar Pradesh may be mentioned. The accused was tried for the murder of the deceased by shooting him with a country made pistol. A cartridge was found near the bed of the deceased. The accused was arrested at a distance of 14 miles from the village which was the place of occurrence. He produced a pistol from his house which indicated that he could alone have known of its existence there. The fire-arms expert proved that it was the same pistol from which the shot was fired and deceased was killed. The Hon'ble Supreme Court while convicting the accused held "Circumstantial Evidence has established that the death of the deceased was caused by the accused and no one else. "

Judicial Witness & Non-Judicial Witness

Judicial Evidence

Evidence deposed in court of justice in proof or disproof of facts is called judicial evidence. The confession made by the accused in the court is also included in judicial evidence. Statements of witnesses and documentary evidence and facts for the examination by the court are also Judicial Evidence.

Non-Judicial Evidence

Any confession made by the accused outside the court in the presence of any person or the admission of a party are called Non-Judicial Evidence, if proved in the court in the form of Judicial Evidence.

CLASSIFICATION OF WITNESSES

There are various classification of witnesses. It is desirable to understand their nature and the impact that they make on any case.

Eye Witness & Hearsay Witness

Eye Witness

A witness who gives testimony to facts seen by him is called an eye witness; an eye witness is a person who saw the act, fact or transaction to which he testifies. An eye witness must be competent (legally fit) and qualified to give witness. A witness who was intoxicated or insane at the time the event occurred is prevented from testifying, regardless of whether he or she was the only eyewitness to the occurrence. Eye witness is given a very high evidentiary value. The Apex Court has remarked in a case that "it is a platitude to say that witnesses have to be weighed and not counted since quality matters more than quantity in human affairs." A single good and honest eye witness is sufficient to prove the charge. It is generally maintained that where a case hangs on the evidence of a single eye witness it may be enough to sustain the conviction given sterling testimony of a competent, honest man. However, as a rule of prudence courts call for corroboration. Therefore, the interest of the eye witness in the prosecution must be examined. This does not, however, mean that in the absence of a corroboration a sterling eye witness should be given any less importance in deciding a case.

Hearsay Witness

Hearsay witness is reported evidence of a witness which he has not seen himself but heard it from others about the occurrence of the incident or fact which he testifies in his witness. Hearsay Evidence is that evidence which the witness has neither personally seen or heard, nor has he perceived through his senses and has come to know about it through some third person. There is no bar to receive hearsay evidence provided it has reasonable nexus and credibility. Hearsay witness has, however, very weak evidentiary value. Hearsay evidence is to be very judiciously kept aside because when a piece of evidence is such that there is no prima facie assurance of its credibility, it would be most risky to act upon it.

In *Lim Yam Yong v. Lam Choon & Co.,AIR 1958 PC 127,,* The Hon'ble Bombay High Court adjudged "Hearsay Evidence which ought to have been rejected as irrelevant does not become admissible as against a party merely because his council fails to take objection when the evidence is tendered."

Hostile Witness & Interested Witness

Hostile Witness

The witness who makes statements adverse to the party calling and examining him is called a hostile witness. A hostile witness may, with the permission of the court or adjudicating authority, be cross examined by the party that has called the witness. The witness of a hostile witness may not be summarily rejected. The evidentiary value of a hostile witness is weighed properly. *In Bhagwan Singh v. State of Haryana,*AIR 1976 SC 202, the court held that merely because the Court gave permission to the Public Prosecutor to cross-examine his own witness describing him as hostile witness does not completely efface his evidence. The evidence remains admissible in the trial and there is no legal bar to base conviction upon the testimony of such witness. *In State of U.P. v, Ramesh Prasad Misra* the Court held that the evidence of a hostile witness would not be totally rejected if spoken in favour of the prosecution or accused, but it can be subjected to close scrutiny and that portion of the evidence which is consistent with the case of the prosecution or defence may be accepted. *In Balu Sonba Shinde v. State of Maharashtra, 2003 SCC (Crl.) 112*, the Supreme Court held that the declaration of a witness to be hostile does not *ipso facto* reject the evidence. The portion of evidence being advantageous to the parties may be taken advantage of, but the Court should be extremely cautious and circumspect in such acceptance. The testimony of hostile witness has to be tested, weighed and considered in the same manner in which the evidence of any other witness in the case.

Interested Witness

An interested witness is that witness who has his own interests involved in giving the witness either in favour of the defence or prosecution. The knowledge of the fact or occurrence which an interested witness deposes before an adjudicating authority may be direct or indirect. For example, an eye witness can also be an interested witness. A hearsay witness can also be an interested witness.

Expert Witness

An 'expert' is not a 'witness' of fact. His evidence, in reality, is of an advisory character. The duty of an 'expert witness' is to furnish the judge with the necessary scientific criteria for testing the accuracy of the conclusion so as to enable the judge to form his independent judgment by the application of this criteria to the facts proved by the evidence of the case. The scientific opinion evidence, if intelligible, convincing and tested becomes a factor, and along with the other evidence of the case helps in reaching a conclusion. The credibility of such a witness depends on the reasons stated in support of his conclusions and the data furnished which form the basis of his conclusions.

SUMMARY OF DISCUSSION

Evidence and witnesses are very necessary to reach at a conclusion in any disputing matter. It helps the judging authority to reach at a verdict. It is always advisable to weigh the evidences, form a definite conclusion based on rationale thinking, and then arrive at a judgment based only on facts in hand.

CONSIDERATION IN DOMESTIC OR DEPARTMENTAL ENQUIRY

As mentioned earlier, strict rules of Evidence Act are not applicable in cases of quasi-judicial nature, or domestic enquiry. But, a casual reference of the important terms relating to evidences and witnesses was necessary to understand the importance of any particular evidence or a witness or the value that must be assigned to them in deciding a case.

In domestic enquiry the cases are not decided on the basis of 'beyond all reasonable doubt' as in case of a criminal prosecution in a law court, but on the basis of 'preponderance of evidence'. The judge in a criminal law suit gives benefit of doubt to the accused. The age old legal theory is that a thousand culprits can be acquitted, but no innocent person should be punished. But, in domestic enquiry an enquiry officer cannot give benefit of doubt to a delinquent employee.

In domestic enquiry a 'Preponderance of evidence' is held sufficient to decide a case. This means a logical conclusion or probability which a rational person can draw by weighing the evidences can become basis for deciding the guilt of a delinquent employee. In other words, the preponderance is based on the more convincing evidence and its probable truth or accuracy only. This does not however mean that a delinquent employee can be held guilty on speculation or surmise. A logical derivative from the materials on record is essential to prove the charge.

It is because, it is only on the basis of evidence adduced during the enquiry that the person facing the enquiry may effectively exercise his right of being heard in respect of the charges against him by showing that charges have not been established and the penalty of dismissal, removal or reduction in rank is not justified. *Dilip Singh Rana v. State of U.P. , 1994 Lab IC 491 (All) (DR).*

In domestic enquiry,the enquiry officer first looks at the direct evidence which is reliable. A single eye witness on which no reasonable doubt can be placed is sufficient to decide a case. However, it always appears more easy in theory than in practice because direct evidence cannot always be available which can straightway help in arriving at a conclusion. When direct evidence is not available the enquiry officer places importance on circumstantial evidence. The enquiry officer can base his findings on circumstantial evidence. Govinda Reddy v. State of Mysore, AIR 1960 SC 29; Deonandan Misra v. State of Bihar, (1955) 2 SCR 570: AIR 1955 SC 801.

For deciding case on circumstantial evidence the enquiry officer assures that the primary facts are proved by credible evidence. Primary facts are basic tenets of the guilt to be proved. There should not be any doubt in this regard. Then inferences are drawn from primary facts leading to consistently proving the hypothesis of the guilt of the person. A chain of evidences lead to the belief that the accused cannot be anybody else but the charge-sheeted employee only. If this inference can be conclusively and reasonably drawn, then there cannot be any hesitation in holding the employee guilty of the charge. The important thing is that the enquiry officer should never considers any evidence or any witness insignificant. It may help in connecting a missing link.

There are some important rules for weighing evidences which the enquiry officer must always follow to avoid any error in judgement-

(a) Direct evidences are of primary importance in deciding the case. But, they should not be heavily relied on. Some corroborative fact must be looked for.

(b) Demeanour of witnesses must be noted down separately. It may not be fresh in mind after a lapse of time when it comes to evaluation of the witnesses.

(c) Importance should not be attached on any witness based on his status.

(d) Written explanation and statement of the charge-sheeted employee throws sufficient light to draw important conclusions.

(e) There may be incompetence of the charge-sheeted employee in cross-examining the prosecution witnesses. Focus must be on to what extent the prosecution satisfactorily proves the charge. The enquiry Officer should not fill gaps in prosecution.

(f) An accomplice witness may try to shift the burden of guilt on the other accused. His deposition needs corroboration.

(g) The witness of a partisan witness needs to be corroborated.

(h) The witness of a hostile witness needs to be corroborated. It is not unworthy,however.

(i) Extraneous matters or personal knowledge should not supplement any evidence on record.

(j) Ascertaining of motive is not required.

The important thing is that the enquiry officer must give a reasoned report after properly weighing the evidences.

An employee cannot be held guilty on suspicion or surmises. Union of India v. S.C.Goel, AIR 1964 SC 364; Gian Mahanti v. State of Maharashtra, (1971) 2 SCC 611; Sripati Ranjan Biswas v. Collector of Customs, AIR 1964 Cal. 415.

CHAPTER VI
PROCEDURE OF DOMESTIC ENQUIRY

The procedure of domestic enquiry is a quasi-judicial procedure. The theory of natural justice is followed at every step of the enquiry. The process of domestic enquiry commences with framing charge on the delinquent employee and concludes with submission of the report of enquiry to the disciplinary authority. We shall discuss the procedure of the enquiry in detail for a lucid comprehension of the subject.

WHO CAN CONDUCT AN ENQUIRY

Normally, it is said that the competent authority can conduct enquiry. But, who is a competent authority, and what invests such competence in him, needs to be understood properly.

The employer who appoints a person has the right to dismiss that person from service. The appointing authority is always a competent punishing authority. Therefore, the appointing authority is competent to conduct an enquiry, and also to pass an order of punishment on the guilt of the employee. The appointing authority may be the employer himself or any other authority down the line in management who is entrusted with the powers to make appointments on behalf of the employer.

The Appointing authority may delegate the powers relating to matters of employee discipline to appropriate levels in the organization for different levels or grades of employees working in the organization. *The authority that is invested with such disciplinary powers is called disciplinary authority. A disciplinary authority may conduct an enquiry and pass an order of punishment on the guilt of an employee.* The disciplinary authority is always a competent punishing authority. However, the power to pass ultimate punishment of dismissal or discharge may or may not rest with the disciplinary authority. It depends on to what extent powers have been delegated to the disciplinary authority by the appointing authority in matters of employee discipline. Sometimes, the appointing authority retains the power to inflict ultimate punishment of discharge or dismissal. *In such case, the disciplinary authority can himself conduct an enquiry and pass punishment orders, except the ultimate punishment of dismissal or discharge of the employee.*

The appointing Authority or the disciplinary authority, as the case may be, on occasions delegate the power to conduct enquiry and verify the charge of misconduct on any delinquent employee on any other person, whether from inside the organization or outside. *That appointed authority is called Enquiry Officer. The Enquiry Officer conducts enquiry on the delegated powers of the appointing authority or the disciplinary authority. The sole work of an enquiry officer is to conduct an enquiry and verify the charge of misconduct on the delinquent employee. The enquiry officer submits his findings of the enquiry to the punishing authority. The job of enquiry officer ends when he submits the report of the enquiry to the punishing authority.*

It may be mentioned that on occasions, depending on the Rules and Regulations of the Organizations or the Standing Orders of the Company, *the disciplinary authority may appoint an enquiry committee consisting of more than one enquiry officer*, but normally not more than two or three persons, to hold enquiry into the charges levelled against a delinquent employee.

Thus, an enquiry can be conducted by-

(a) The Appointing Authority, or

(b) The Disciplinary Authority, or

(c) The Enquiry Officer (or, The Enquiry Committee)

The enquiry becomes invalid and bad in the eyes of law if any incompetent person holds the enquiry. *S. Parthasarathi v. State of A.P.,(1974) 3 SCC 459.*

The punishing authority i.e., the appointing authority or the disciplinary authority, delegates it's power to conduct enquiry to Enquiry Officer for administrative convenience.

In the case of *Pradyut Kumar v. Chief Justice of Calcutta High Court, AIR 1956, SC 285,* the Hon'ble Supreme Court had maintained that the exercise of the power to appoint or dismiss an officer is the exercise not of the judicial power but administrative power. However, an opportunity to show-cause and an enquiry simulating judicial standards has to precede the exercise thereof. A functionary who has to decide an administrative matter, such as the dismissal of the member of a staff, can obtain the material on which he is to act in such manner as may be feasible and convenient, provided only that affected party has a fair opportunity to correct or contradict any relevant and prejudicial matter.

The rules regarding appointment of an enquiry officer as mentioned in the rules and regulations or the Standing Orders of the organization must be strictly adhered. The violation of the rules has the potential to invalidate the enquiry.

An outsider, whether a labour consultant or an advocate, can be appointed as enquiry officer only when the rules specifically mentions about the same.

The appointment of an outsider as the enquiry officer does not vitiate the enquiry. *Md. Abdul Kadar v. Royal Auto Supply Company, 1964 ICR 751 (IT).*

It cannot be presumed that since a labour consultant or an advocate is paid by the employer he would be biased in conducting enquiry. *Saran Motors v. Vishwanath, (1964) II LLJ 139 (SC).*

QUALIFICATIONS THAT AN ENQUIRY OFFICER SHOULD POSSESS

An enquiry officer should be an independent, unbiased person who should have good knowledge of the rules and regulations of the organizations. Preferably, he should be properly trained in conducting quasi-judicial enquiry, either by formal training or experience.

If any officer has any bias which may be due to personal knowledge of the case, or he is witness in the case, or he has any kind of interest or any leaning, then he does not qualify to hold the enquiry.

An iota of doubt about the biasness of the enquiry officer is sufficient to vitiate the case. *Ramniwas Sharma v. Union Of India, (1983) Lab IC 828 (Gau HC); LIC of India v. Mohan Lal Saraf, (1978) 2 SLR 868 (J&K HC).*

Personal Knowledge of the case or any kind of personal interest in the case creates a bias on the part of the authority who decides the case. *GopalKrishna v. State, AIR 1964, All 481.*

In cases of domestic enquiry the Punishing Authority appoints the enquiry officer to independently and fairly hold an enquiry into a charge of misconduct. The same Punishing Authority appoints a Presiding Officer to prove the charge of misconduct. The delinquent employee, therefore, suspects that the enquiry officer would toe on the lines of the management. Even a small doubt of bias, therefore, makes the delinquent dejected towards the enquiry, and he loses faith in the process. It requires tremendous amount of goodwill and impartiality on the part of an enquiry officer to win the confidence of the delinquent employee as well as the employer.

Appointment of an enquiry officer requires formal appointment in writing. The charge-sheet may also contain in some cases the name of the enquiry officer.

The principle of natural justice demands that the officer conducting enquiry should not be rigidly interested in proving the guilt of the accused. *A.R.S. Choudhary v. Union Of India, AIR 1956 ,Cal 662.*

COMMENCEMENT OF THE PROCEEDINGS

The punishing authority hands over the papers relating to the enquiry to the enquiry officer. It contains copy of the charge-sheet, complaint letter on which the charge-sheet is based, other relevant papers like, copy of the appointment of the management representative, reply furnished by the charge-sheeted employee in response to the charge-sheet, etc.

The enquiry officer commences enquiry as per date, place and time of enquiry mentioned in the charge-sheet. In some charge-sheets the information about the enquiry officer and schedule of enquiry is not mentioned in the charge-sheet. In that case the communication regarding the schedule of enquiry to the charge-sheeted employee becomes the responsibility of the enquiry officer.

When the delinquent employee is not in suspension-pending enquiry then the intimation of the date of enquiry is communicated to the charge-sheeted employee through proper channel, ie., officially through his superior authority. When the charge-sheeted employee is under suspension pending enquiry then communication of the schedule of enquiry is assured through postal dispatch of the schedule of enquiry by registered post with acknowledgement due. Nowadays, electronic mode of communications are also used. The only requirement is that proper proof of dispatch and receipt or, non receipt, of the communication could be placed in record in the document form. Since different modes of service of charge-sheet to the delinquent employee has been discussed earlier the same will not be repeated. Suffice to say here that before commencement of the enquiry it is the duty of the enquiry officer to ensure proper communication of the schedule of enquiry to the charge-sheeted employee, and other persons concerned with the enquiry.

The enquiry commences when all concerned persons report for the enquiry at the appointed date, place and time. The enquiry officer ensures that all the persons required at the enquiry are present, i.e., the delinquent or the charge-sheeted employee and the management representative to represent the case of the management. Co-worker to assist the delinquent, the investigating Officer, if any, or witnesses appear at the enquiry, as required.

INITIAL QUESTIONS/COMMUNICATION TO THE CHARGE-SHEETED EMPLOYEE

Communication and explaining the charges levelled on the employee

Irrespective of the fact that the charge-sheeted employee has received, read and understood the charge-sheet and gave his explanation to the charge-sheet, the enquiry officer must begin the enquiry by reading over and explaining the charges to the delinquent authority. No presumption should withhold the enquiry officer from proceeding at the beginning of the enquiry in a different manner. Invariably, the charge-sheet should be read over, explained and exhibited. *The author has always preferred the charge-sheet to be made the first exhibit in a domestic enquiry proceeding.*

Reading over and explaining the explanation of the Charge-sheet

If the explanation to the charge-sheet has been given by the charge-sheeted employee then it should be read over and explained to the charge-sheeted employee. It should be explained to the charge-sheeted employee that since his explanation of the charge-sheet has not been found satisfactory by the charge-sheet issuing authority hence this has been decided by the management to proceed with the enquiry. *The explanation of the charge-sheeted employee should be properly exhibited.*

Communication about the appointment of the Enquiry Officer and the Management Representative

The charge-sheeted employee should be communicated at the beginning of the enquiry itself regarding appointment of the management representative by the punishing authority to lead the prosecution witnesses. The letter of authorization appointing the management representative must be shown to the charge-sheeted employee, and contents thereof should be read over and explained. *The said letter of authorization should be exhibited.*

In case, the charge-sheet itself did not contain the information regarding the appointment of enquiry officer, and it was subsequently decided, then *the letter of authorization mentioning the appointment of enquiry officer should also be shown to the charge-sheeted employee and properly exhibited.*

Admission of the guilt may be questioned in the beginning

At this point of time the enquiry officer can ask the charge-sheeted employee if the charge-sheeted employee admits the charges levelled against him or not. If the charge-sheeted employee admits the guilt, then the full circle of enquiry is not followed. In such a case, the charge-sheeted employee makes his statement first, and pleads guilty. The guilty pleading statement of the charge-sheeted employee is recorded by the enquiry officer and counter sign of the charge-sheeted employee is taken in the proceedings. The Management Representative also signs on that statement. This is followed by opportunity given to the management representative to cross-examine or question the charge-sheeted employee , if he so wishes.

It may be mentioned that the management, and the delinquent both repose their faith on the enquiry officer as an independent person. It is duty of the enquiry officer to find the facts at the enquiry, and base his findings on that, to see that the charges levelled against the delinquent are proved or not. But, at the same time he has not to unnecessarily lengthen the enquiry. Hence, in cases of misconduct of not very serious nature, the option of asking the delinquent employee whether he accepts the charges or not may be judiciously applied.

The Rule that the worker cannot be examined in the beginning is not applicable when the worker admits the guilt before the commencement of the enquiry. In that case his statement must be recorded first to provide him an opportunity to explain his misconduct. When the worker admits the guilt then asking the management to lead evidence against him to prove the allegation is mere an empty formality. *Central Bank of India v. Karunamoy Bannerjee,(1966) 2 LLJ 739: (1967) 15 FLR 318 (SC).*

The purpose of enquiry is to find out if the charges levelled against the charge-sheeted employee are correct or not. If the charge-sheeted employee pleads guilty at the beginning itself, there is no point in running the full circle of enquiry proceeding. However, such guilt admissions are not very common at the beginning of the enquiry. Moreover, the enquiry officer has to be very careful while recording the admission of the guilt or confession of the employee.

In *Ramlal v. Union of India (AIR 1962, Raj 57),* the watchman Ramlal, in reply to the charge-sheet craved mercy on the ground that this was the first occurrence during his service for eleven years, pointing out at the same time the difficulties of a watchman escorting the train at night in detecting a preplanned theft of goods carried by rail on the track. He was dismissed from service without formal enquiry on the ground that it was admission of guilt with a conditional apology. Their Lordships set aside the order of dismissal observing that when it was "not a clear and unambiguous admission of guilt, the employer should have held a formal enquiry, before dismissing the watchman".

On some occasions a charge-sheeted employee after admission of the guilt in the enquiry may subsequently claim that the admission of guilt was under undue duress. It is also contended that the duty of the enquiry officer is only to confirm the charges levelled against the delinquent employee based on the material facts and records. Therefore, question regarding admission of guilt to the delinquent employee at the beginning of the enquiry is meaningless, particularly in view of the fact that the enquiry begins only after delinquent's explanation to the charge-sheet is considered unacceptable by the charge-sheet issuing authority. However, it must also be noted that the enquiry proceeds in that case also where the charge-sheeted employee does not tender any explanation to the charge-sheet and decides to defend himself at the enquiry only. Moreover, the question regarding admission of guilt provides an opportunity to know the opinion of the delinquent employee. Therefore, an enquiry officer can safely put this initial question to the delinquent employee.

The charge-sheeted employee, however, should not be very probingly interrogated at the beginning of the enquiry. This may vitiate the enquiry. A few initial questions not of very snooping nature may however be asked in the beginning of the enquiry. After all, an enquiry cannot start in a very mechanical form.

Option to take help of a co-worker must be asked at the beginning.

At the very outset, the enquiry officer must ask the charge-sheeted employee if he needs any assistance at the enquiry of a co-worker who would assist the charge-sheeted employee at the enquiry. If the Charge-sheeted employee replies in affirmative, then a request is sent by the enquiry officer to the concerned departmental head to whose department the co-worker belongs to release the co-worker to assist the charge-sheeted employee at the enquiry. Normally, such request is acceded to by the management. As the term co-worker suggests, the co-worker ideally belong to the department of the delinquent employee. He can be a Union representative of that department as well.

It may be noted here that attendance of co-worker at the enquiry cannot be forced on the co-worker whom the delinquent employee wishes to be present at the enquiry. It should be willingness of the co-worker, as well. Else, a different choice is asked by the delinquent employee. If the co-worker chooses to be present during the enquiry proceedings with the charge-sheeted employee then the enquiry should normally not proceed in his absence. The co-worker of the delinquent also signs on all the documents and records in the enquiry.

The presence of the co-worker at the enquiry must be ensured in accordance with the provisions mentioned in the Rules and regulations and Standing Orders of the Organization.

The decision of the charge-sheeted employee either to avail or not to avail the assistance of the co-worker at the enquiry is required to be mentioned in the proceedings without fail.

Language to be adopted must be communicated citing Rules and Regulations

At the beginning of the enquiry itself the enquiry officer must make it clear to the delinquent employee about the language to be adopted in the enquiry procedure. The use of English language is generally acceptable in the enquiry if the proceedings and recordings are explained to the charge-sheeted workman in the language understood by him. Sometimes, the rules and regulations of the Organization or the Standing Orders also provide specific instructions in this regard. Such specific instructions if not followed may be held bad in the eyes of law.

The depositions when made in vernacular language are translated into English and then recorded by the enquiry officer. It is abundant duty of the enquiry officer to explain the translated version to the charge-sheeted employee in the language understood by him. Otherwise, the enquiry is vitiated.

The pressing demand of the workman to conduct the enquiry in vernacular language, without any specific instruction in this regard in the Standing Orders or Rules of the organization, is often tackled by the enquiry officers by making the delinquent understand that the purpose of providing a co-worker at the enquiry is also intended to cover the gap of language barrier in the enquiry. *An enquiry cannot get vitiated only because the unreasonable demand of the workman to conduct the enquiry in the vernacular language was not accepted by the enquiry officer. Management of Britannia Biscuits Co. Ltd., v. Workmen Del. Gaz., dt. 14.12.1972. p. 801 (L.C.); Harikisan v. State of Maharashtra AIR 1962 SC 911.*

Communication of the process of enquiry in the beginning

The enquiry officer should explain the process of enquiry to the charge-sheeted employee as well as to other concerned persons present during the enquiry. The enquiry officer must not presume that the charge-sheeted employee or the management representative is aware about the procedure to be followed in the enquiry. *Explaining the procedure of enquiry at the beginning of the enquiry should be done without fail. The author always explained the process of enquiry in brief before every domestic enquiry in the below mentioned manner:*

"The burden of proof lies on the management and the management representative would first get the opportunity to make his statement regarding the charges levelled on the employee. The charge-sheeted employee would get opportunity to cross-examine or counter question the management representative in connection with the statement made by him at the enquiry relating to the charges. This would be followed by presentation of the management witnesses one by one, and the charge=sheeted employee would get opportunity to cross examine the management witnesses one by one. A witness would not be produced at the enquiry in the presence of the another witness. When all the management witnesses are over, opportunity would be given to the charge-sheeted employee to make his statement. This would be followed by cross-examination of the charge-sheeted employee by the management representative. Next, the charge-

sheeted employee would present the witnesses from his side one by one, and the management representative would get opportunity to cross-examine them one by one. All the material facts relating to the charge would be presented at the enquiry and exhibited properly. The enquiry would be conducted without any prejudice or bias to any side."

The content may be followed in spirit as it explains in brief the process to be followed in a normal domestic enquiry.

RECORDING OF THE PROCEEDINGS OF THE ENQUIRY: BEGIN WITH ATTENDANCE

Before recording any deposition at the enquiry attendance should be invariably recorded. Attendance recording is mandatory. It should be properly recorded and duly signed with date.

No unauthorized person should be allowed at the enquiry

The presence of any unauthorized person should not be allowed at the place of enquiry. The charge-sheeted employee may claim the influence of the unauthorized person on the enquiry officer if they are allowed to be present at the enquiry. This is also avoided because the depositions at the enquiry may be communicated to persons who are in a position to influence the enquiry. It is the duty of the enquiry officer to ensure that no unauthorized person is present at the place of enquiry. If any unauthorized person is present then the charge-sheeted employee may insist that his attendance should also be mentioned in the daily order sheet or proceedings of the enquiry. Else, he can refuse to take part in the enquiry.

An example how to begin the proceedings of the enquiry has been mentioned below:

"Enquiry proceedings into the charge-sheet Reference Number___ bearing date__ issued to the charge-sheeted employee Mr.___bearing employee identification number__ designated as __ in the grade__in ___department of the Company.

Date of Enquiry___
Place of Enquiry__
Time of Enquiry__

Persons Present

1. Mr. _____(Enquiry Officer) (Signature)
2. Mr._____(Other Member, in case of an Enquiry Committee) (Signature)
3. Mr._____(Other Member, in case of an Enquiry Committee) (Signature)
4. Mr. _____(Charge-sheeted Employee) (Signature)
5. Mr._____(Co=worker) (Signature)
6. Mr. _____(The Management Representative) (Signature)
7. Mr._____(Any other relevant person like, a witness) (Signature)

(In fact, every time this process of taking attendance is followed when the enquiry begins after an adjournment whatsoever may be the duration of the adjournment.)

Proceedings of the enquiry follow recording of the attendance for the day.

_____

_____

_____

_____

_____

At the bottom of each page the signature of the persons present at the enquiry should be invariably taken. Otherwise, the charge-sheeted employee may claim that page has been changed to the prejudice of the delinquent employee.

Before taking the signature of the charge-sheeted employee and others the contents of the page should be read over and explained to the charge-sheeted employee, and the same should also be recorded, like " *the abovementioned depositions at the enquiry were read over and explained to the charge-sheeted employee in the language understood by him and he confirmed to have understood the same.* "

There should be some example or evidence to show that the statements were explained to the workers. *Thomas Mouget & Company v. Workmen Cal. Gaz. Part IC. dt. 15.12.1968, p. 175 (IT).*

When the statements of witnesses were not read over to the opposite party and in any case they were not explained in the language which he understood, then the enquiry is defective. *Aswini Kumar & Co. v. Workmen Cal. Gaz., Part IC, dt. .07.08.1969, p. 851 (IT).*

Recording of the enquiry proceedings should be proper and date wise

The enquiry officer should himself record the proceedings of the enquiry. *The proceedings are generally recorded in narrative form.* However, depending on the rules in this regard the assistance of a clerk/typist is permitted. The enquiry proceedings should be recorded date wise in sequence. *Exhibits should also be mentioned in proper serial order.* It is because in the report of the enquiry the summary of the enquiry proceedings is also mentioned. In case, the proceedings are not properly mentioned in sequence date wise then question may arise how did the enquiry officer evaluate the depositions in the enquiry. It may, therefore, vitiate the enquiry.

RECORDING OF STATEMENTS AND CROSS-EXAMINATIONS

After recording introductory formalities statements and cross-examinations begin which form very important part of the enquiry proceedings.

Statement and cross examination of Management Representative

The recording of the statements begin with recording the statement of the management representative as mentioned in the enquiry proceedings earlier.

When the charge-sheeted employee is examined in the beginning of the enquiry then it constitutes a serious flaw in the enquiry.

In the case of *Associated Cement Company Ltd. v. Workmen, (1963) 7 FLR 269: (1963) 2 LLJ 396 (SC),* the Apex Court mentioned that the proper procedure in departmental enquiries is to first lead evidence against the workman charged, give an opportunity to the workman to cross examine the said witnesses and then the workman should be asked whether he wants to give any explanation about the evidence led against him. *The management representative gives the list of witnesses to be produced by the management either in the part of his statement, or after making his statement.*

After the statement of the management representative is over, the charge-sheeted employee gets opportunity to cross examine the management representative followed by statement of prosecution witnesses and their cross examination, one by one.

Cross Examination of Management Representative or other Witnesses by the Charge-sheeted employee

The charge-sheeted employee gets opportunity to cross-examine the management representative or the prosecution witnesses. The charge sheeted employee may or may not avail the opportunity to cross-examine when such opportunity is given to him. The charge-sheeted employee is not obliged to state the reason for not cross-examining either management representative or any particular witness. He may simply decline. However, on every occasion when the opportunity is so given it should be recorded in the proceeding. An example has been shown below:

"The charge-sheeted employee was provided the opportunity to cross examine the _____ but the charge-sheeted employee declined to avail the opportunity to cross-examine the _____."

The abovementioned deposition relating to cross-examination of _____ was recorded and explained to the charge sheeted employee in the language understood by him, and he confirmed to have understood the same.

The signature of the charge-sheeted employee and other concerned persons present in the enquiry should be taken here.

The List of the Prosecution Witnesses should be disclosed to the delinquent employee

The theory of natural justice requires that the information about the witnesses must be provided so that the other party can make adequate preparations for cross-examination. This is all the more required in domestic enquiry because the delinquent employee is generally not properly trained or knowledgeable in this respect. All reasonable opportunity for cross-examination should be provided to the delinquent employee. *Union of India v. Ravi Dutt,(1973)I SLR 1222 (Del HC).*

The enquiry officer must give an opportunity to the delinquent workmen to cross-examine the management witness. *Sur Enamel & Stamping Works v. Workmen, (1961) 2 LLJ 367 (SC); Khem Chand v. Union Of India, AIR 1958 SC 300; Union of India v. T. R. Verma, (1958) SCR 499: AIR 1957 SC 882.*

A witness should be cross-examined immediately after his deposition at the enquiry.

Statement of witnesses can be recorded in question answer form, when the management representative puts question to them while examination, or narrative form, when they give witness in simple statement form; but recording of cross-examination cannot be in narration form.

The cross-examination part must be recorded in question and answer form only.

For example, during cross –examination recording of the questions and answer should be done in following manner:

Cross Examination of Mr._____,the Management Representative(MR); Or, Mr._____,the Management Witness (MW) No _____ , as the case may be, by the Charge –sheeted employee Mr. _____.

CS employee: Did you see me keeping the stolen material in my scooter? MW: Yes, I saw it myself.

CS employee: How big was the material? MW: It was of the size of a cricket ball.

CS employee: What was the time then? MW: 6.30 pm.

CS employee: From how far you saw me ? MW: I saw it from a distance of about 20 yards.

CS employee: How do you come to the Works? MW: I live in the nearby colony. I come walking on foot.

CS employee: What were you doing in scooter stand? MW: I had gone there by chance since the tea break had started.

CS employee: What was the date? MW: 12th of December. I was in 'B' Shift on that day.

CS employee: Was the visibility clear in the December evening, or it was dark?

MW: It was almost dark but parking light was on.

CS employee: Can you see specific item of the size of a cricket ball in dim parking light and identify the material ?

MW: Yes.

CS employee: No further questions.

The enquiry officer confirmed that the charge-sheeted employee had no further questions to ask.

The above mentioned cross-examination was concluded when the charge sheeted employee confirmed that he had no further questions to ask. (*This part should never be forgotten; The enquiry officer must confirm that the delinquent had no further questions to ask.*)

"*The abovementioned recording was read and explained to the charge-sheeted employee in the language understood by him, and the charge-sheeted employee confirmed to have understood the same.*" *This is signed, with date by all the members present at the enquiry.*

Not Signing the enquiry proceedings by the delinquent is not disobedience or misconduct

If the charge-sheeted employee does not sign on enquiry proceedings, or if any witness refuses to sign on any proceeding then it does not become a case of disobedience or a misconduct. On many occasions the charge-sheeted employee although does not run away from the enquiry, but he refuses to sign on enquiry proceedings.

The enquiry officer need not put any pressure on the charge-sheeted employee to sign on enquiry proceedings. He should note down the fact that "*the charge-sheeted employee was present during the enquiry but he declined to sign on the enquiry proceedings. This was read over and explained in the language understood by the charge-sheeted employee.*" All the members present at the enquiry should sign the proceedings along with this notation.

Ideally, however, the charge-sheeted employee is required to sign at the end of the proceedings every day, and a witness must sign after he deposed at the enquiry.

A witness can refer to prepared notes

It is permissible, and reasonable, for a witness to refer to a prepared notes. It is because in case of lengthy statements and time gap between occurrence and enquiry may make it difficult for even a genuine witness to depose all the details correctly and without any miss. However, if it appears to the enquiry officer that it is prepared by somebody else on behalf of the witness, and it is tutored to give a false witness then he may prohibit the witness from referring to such notes. The language of the witness and demeanor of the witness may provide a good hint to the enquiry officer in this regard.

A witness may be re-examined and cross -examined.

A witness may be re-examined and cross-examined. However, the purpose of such re-examination should be to clarify any point in the statement, or for verification of any deposition. A re-examination or a cross-examination should not be allowed to fill a gap in the prosecution.

Each time a worker is called for re-examination, an opportunity for cross-examination should be provided to the other party.

The enquiry officer must hear the witnesses himself.

The enquiry officer must hear the witnesses himself. He cannot delegate the task of hearing the witnesses to someone else. *Amulya Kumar Sidkar v. L. M. Bakshi, AIR 1958, Cal. 470.*

The enquiry officer cannot ask leading questions to the delinquent employee

The enquiry officer cannot ask leading questions to the delinquent employee. Though, asking a few questions for the purpose of clarification of any point does not come under the category of leading questions. But, if the questions are probing in nature and they are directed towards hinting the guilt of the employees then such leading questions are capable of showing bias on the part of the enquiry officer which can vitiate the enquiry. *Ram Netra v. Deputy Superintendent of Police, (1966) I LLJ 363: AIR 1966 ,MP 58.*

When the enquiry officer makes a special attempt to make out a case against the workman and assumes the additional role of a prosecutor then this vitiates the enquiry. *Alembic Chemical Works Co. Ltd., Baroda v. Bhikuram, 1954, ICR 588.*

Admission of documents and other real evidences in the enquiry

All the documents and real evidences must be properly exhibited that are directly connected with the case. A document does not get the status of an evidence merely because it is presented by a party in the enquiry. The truth of the content of the document must be proved by the person presenting it, and it must pass the test of a cross-examination by the other party. Besides, the party presenting it must clarify as to how does it relate to the matter of fact.

The real evidence is an impersonal evidence or a material evidence connected with the case. For example, a recovered stolen material unless and until presented in the enquiry along with a copy of the FIR containing the description of the said material cannot get the status of a real evidence to be relied upon. It must also be subject to a cross-examination.

All documents and real evidences presented at the enquiry must be properly exhibited and numbered in serial of their production at the enquiry.

Statement by the Charge-sheeted employee , defence witnesses and their cross-examination

After all the witnesses of the prosecution side is over, the enquiry officer should give opportunity to the charge-sheeted employee to make his statement, if he so wishes. In case the charge-sheeted employee refuses to make any statement, it should be accordingly recorded in the proceedings.

The Enquiry Officer may not allow the charge-sheeted employee to submit a written statement.

It is not required on the part of the charge-sheeted employee to submit a written statement. He can, however, refer to written notes for refreshing his memory. The proper procedure is to read out the document rather than produce it as an exhibit. This is applied to charge-sheeted employee or any other witness making a deposition at the enquiry. *Kanti Prasad Jayshankar v. Purushottamdas Ranchhoddas Yagnik, (1969) I SCC 455.*

The charge-sheeted employee after his deposition is subject to cross –examination by the management representative.

A workman should be given fair opportunity to examine and cross-examine witnesses, including himself. *Central Bank of India Ltd. v. Karunamoy Bannerjee, (1967) 2 LLJ 739: (1967) 15 FLR 398 (SC); Firestone Tyre and Rubber Co. Ltd. v. Workman (1967) 2 LLJ 715.*

Production of witnesses by charge-sheeted employee.

The charge-sheeted employee during the course of his statement, or after that, must submit a list of witnesses to be produced by him. It is duty of the enquiry officer to help the charge-sheeted employee in summoning defence witnesses. However, the enquiry officer does not have the powers to summon a witness like a court of law. At his best, the enquiry officer can request the management to ensure the attendance of the defence witnesses at the enquiry. The request of the enquiry officer is generally acceded to by the management.

Enquiry Officer can refuse any unreasonable demand regarding production of defence witnesses

All Reasonable requests of the delinquent employee is normally accepted by the enquiry officer to ensure fair play and justice in the domestic enquiry. However, if the charge-sheeted employee makes any unreasonable request to the enquiry officer in this regard, then the enquiry officer may reject such requests.

The enquiry officer may turn down the request of the charge-sheeted employee when he presents a long list of defence witnesses, particularly when it is either a dilatory tactics or to harass or embarrass the management unreasonably. If the witnesses have to depose the same fact, then there is no need to present too many witnesses to depose the same fact.

The charge-sheeted employee cannot also press the enquiry officer to present any particular witness from his side when the witness is not willing to appear at the enquiry. It is not duty of the management to present defence witnesses. *Tata Oil Mills Ltd. v. Workmen, (1964) 2 LLJ 113: AIR 1965 SC 155.*

If the charge-sheeted employee presses the enquiry officer to present any outside witness then the enquiry officer may show his inability to present the witness at the enquiry. It is because the outside witnesses are not allowed at the departmental or domestic enquiry.

Whenever any request of the delinquent employee regarding production of a defence witness is refused by the enquiry officer, then proper reason for denial of such request should be given. It is also required to take the matter in proceedings in black and white to avoid any future predicament.

If the enquiry officer purposefully or in a biased manner refuses any defence witness then it constitutes a serious infirmity in the enquiry.

If the refusal to examine a witness or to allow other evidences to be led appears to be the result of the desire on the part of the enquiry officer to deprive the person charged of an opportunity to establish his innocence that of course would be a serious matter. *Anand Bazar Patrika v. Employees, (1963) 2 LLJ 429 (SC); A.R.S. Choudhary v. Union of India, (1957) I LLJ 494 Cal. H.C.*

At the end of the cross-examination of defence witnesses the enquiry officer must confirm from the charge-sheeted employee that he has no more witnesses to be produced. Then only he should consider the cross examination of the defence side as over. *This fact must also be recorded in the proceedings.*

CLOSING OF THE ENQUIRY PROCEEDINGS

Ideally, after the cross examination of the defence witnesses is over, the enquiry proceedings come to an end. However, before closing the enquiry proceedings the enquiry officer must confirm from both the management representative and the delinquent employee if they have something more to add to the enquiry which can help in reaching at a justified conclusion of the enquiry.

When both the prosecution and defence side confirm that they have nothing to add to the enquiry, then only it should be considered to be closed. This fact must be captured in the proceedings of the enquiry duly signed by all the members present.

Ex-party enquiry to be held If the delinquent employee does not co-operate

If the employee does not co-operate at the enquiry, the enquiry may proceed ex-parte. A charged employee may not appear at the enquiry from the first day of the enquiry itself, or he may subsequently withdraw from the enquiry on one pretext or the other.

Before proceeding with the ex-parte enquiry fair opportunity should be given to the employee to participate in the enquiry. It is because, an ex-parte enquiry is not considered as acceptable as the one in which the charged employee takes part in the enquiry proceedings and cross-examines the witnesses and material facts brought at the enquiry. Nonetheless, the charged employee should not be allowed to upset the enquiry process by his hostile approach and non-cooperation at the enquiry.

At least two opportunities must be provided to the charged employee to appear at the enquiry, and proper communication must be made to the employee that in his absence the enquiry would proceed ex-parte for which he alone would be responsible.

Registered letters with acknowledgement due must be sent to the known residential addresses of the employee to ensure that proper communication has been made to the employee. Reasonable time must also be provided vide these letters to allow the employee to participate at the enquiry. Haste in conducting the enquiry ex-parte would raise reasonable doubts on the intention of the management to conduct a fair enquiry.

If on both the occasions, the registered letters sent by the employee returns "undelivered" or with remarks of "Refusal to Accept", then the charge-sheet along with the date of next enquiry must be published in the widely circulated two newspapers for proper communication of the enquiry dates to the charged employee and allowing him to participate at the enquiry. Still, however, the delinquent employee does not turn up for the enquiry then the enquiry may proceed ex-parte.

A domestic enquiry was initiated against a workman after serving of charge-sheet on him. At a particular stage of the enquiry, the workman withdrew from the enquiry. Consequently, without even completing the enquiry ex-parte, in the manner prescribed by the standing orders, the employer dismissed the workman from service for alleged misconduct. Adjudicating upon the industrial dispute, arising out of the dismissal without completing the domestic enquiry in accordance with the relevant provisions of the standing orders was invalid. Affirming the view of the Labour Court in appeal, the Supreme Court observed that, the fact that the workman withdrew from the enquiry at an early stage did not absolve the enquiry officer from concluding the enquiry by taking evidence ex-parte. *Imperial Tobacco Co. of India v. its Workmen, (1961) II LLJ 414 SC: AIR 1962, SC 1348)*

It is not uncommon for the enquiry proceedings to end in ex-parte enquiry.

REPORT WRITING BY THE ENQUIRY OFFICER

After conclusion of the enquiry proceedings the enquiry officer is required to write a report of the enquiry to be presented to the disciplinary authority. The enquiry officer weighs the evidences produced at the enquiry, and based on the material facts deposed at the enquiry, the enquiry officer tries to logically arrive at the conclusion whether the charge levelled against the employee is correct or not. The enquiry officer has to conclusively arrive at this conclusion, and there cannot be any ambiguity in the findings of the enquiry officer.

How the enquiry officer weighs the evidences to arrive at a logical finding has been discussed in chapter V.

The findings of the enquiry officer must depend on evidences and material facts deposed at the enquiry

The findings of the enquiry officer must stand on a sound footing. It should be based on evidences produced at the enquiry in the presence of the charge-sheeted employee and all material facts deposed at the enquiry with charge-sheeted employee properly finding opportunity to cross-examine them, if the enquiry has not proceeded ex-parte.

It is a well settled principle that a document or piece of evidence not included in the memorandum of charges and not disclosed to the party charged cannot be made the foundation of the findings against the delinquent. Such a procedure militates against the principle of natural justice and would vitiate the proceedings. *G.S. Sial v. President of India and others, (1981 Lab IC 59 All).*

In a case the petitioner was dismissed not on charge served on him but on the other facts and circumstances which were never disclosed to him. As he had no opportunity to meet those charges, it was held that, there had been a failure of the principles of natural justice. *Raghabans v. State of Bihar, (AIR 1957 Pat. 100).*

Where the order of dismissal merely stated that from the material on file the authority is of opinion that he is not fit to be retained in service and so he should be removed. It was held that, the order cannot be upheld since it is not a speaking order and so an arbitrary order. *State of Punjab v. Bakhtawar Singh (1972 4 SC 730).*

A workman who is to answer a charge must not only know the accusation but also the testimony by which the accusation is supported. For instance, if a document is relied upon by a witness and also by the enquiry officer in his finding, it must be made available to the workman before he is called upon to the Industrial Tribunal.

In the case of *Tata Iron & Steel Co. v. Central Govt. Industrial Tribunal (1966 II LLJ 749 Pat)*, it was held that withholding of important piece of evidence namely, documents, reports, etc., which have bearing on the charges from the persons charged are sufficient grounds to show that the principles of natural justice have been violated in the domestic enquiry.

If the findings of the enquiry are based on reports given by the superior officers but, such reports are not made available to the concerned workmen nor are the officers made available for cross examination, the enquiry would not be fair and proper. *Sur Enamel & Stamping Work Ltd. v. their Workmen, (1963 IILLJ 361 SC ,per Das Gupta J.*

The Enquiry Officer should not prescribe any punishment in his report.

The enquiry officer should not prescribe any punishment in his report. Punishing a delinquent employee falls within the ambit of Punishing Authority. The enquiry officer should not prescribe any appropriate punishment. *Krishna Chandra Tandon v. Union of India, (1974) 4 SCC 374.*

The Enquiry Officer must specifically write in his report, relating to each charge separately, whether the charge is established or not. On the basis of an ambiguous report the punishing authority cannot take any decision.

The report of the enquiry officer should be properly signed and dated.

It is important to note that there cannot be dissenting report of an enquiry officer when an enquiry committee holds the enquiry. There should be unanimity in decision. The purpose of the enquiry is to assist the punishing authority in arriving at a decision regarding guilt of an accused based on the records of enquiry. The members of the enquiry committee are required to give one single report signed by all the members of the enquiry committee.

CONCLUSION OF THE ENQUIRY

Once the enquiry officer submits his report to the disciplinary officer his job as enquiry officer is considered to be over, and with this the enquiry also concludes.

DISPOSAL OF THE CASE BY THE PUNISHING AUTHORITY

The punishing authority normally takes a decision regarding the punishment to the delinquent employee based on the report of the enquiry and findings of the enquiry officer. The punishing authority, however, can disagree with the findings of the enquiry officer. In that event, the punishing authority can reject the entire report submitted by the enquiry officer and order a fresh enquiry. Otherwise, based on the depositions at the enquiry as mentioned in the enquiry proceedings, the punishing authority may arrive at his own conclusion and award punishment accordingly.

If the punishing authority agrees with the report and findings of the enquiry officer then he is not required to give any reasons for awarding any punishment. If, however, the punishing authority disagrees with the findings of the enquiry officer, then he must record reasons for the same. This is the requirement to pass a 'speaking order' as it has been made essential by the Apex Court.

It is a requirement of the natural justice that the findings of the enquiry officer must be communicated to the delinquent employee before the punishing authority decides on a punishment based on that report. Because, the delinquent employee must have an opportunity to counter and contradict any illogical finding of the enquiry officer.

The punishing authority must himself decide a punishment for the delinquent

The report of the enquiry officer does not contain any suggestion regarding punishment. The enquiry officer has no role to either prescribe or decide on a punishment. This is a special prerogative of the punishing authority. The punishing authority normally decides on the punishment based on the gravity of the offence and past record of the delinquent.

SOME IMPORTANT POINTS REGARDING DOMESTIC ENQUIRY

■ *Enquiry proceedings must be held during normal office hours*

Enquiry proceedings should be conducted during normal office hours. The enquiry officer should not show any deliberate eagerness to complete the enquiry. The enquiry officer should not seem to be in a hurry to complete the enquiry. Enquiry proccedings should not be stretched after working hours of the establishment, and no enquiry should be conducted on a holiday.

In a case the Industrial Tribunal maintained that there are certain concerns which work day and night and in such concern the night time is also included in the normal working hours. When journalists in a newspaper work during night time then holding of enquiry in a newspaper establishment during night time cannot be held to be invalid. *Loksatta v. Workmen, 1958 ICR 187 (IT).*

However, the above mentioned view of the industrial tribunal should be considered as an exception where conducting enquiry during normal working day hours is not possible. It is because, it is not only the newspaper establishment where the journalists work during night, but majority of the factories work during the night shift also and it is not uncommon for the industrial workers to work in night shifts.

It is prudent to stick to the general principle of conducting enquiry proceedings during the normal administrative working hour of the establishment.

■ *Proper entry to and exit from office of employee, suspended pending enquiry, must be ensured by the enquiry officer*

It is the duty of the enquiry officer to ensure proper entry to and exit from office of the suspended employee whenever he comes for the enquiry. Normally, the gate pass or attendance card of the employee is forfeited when he is suspended. Therefore, in factory set-up, or where security arrangements are high, it is difficult for the suspended employee to enter the premises where enquiry is to be held. A proper instruction to the security personnel must reach in advance that at what time and on what date the suspended employee has to enter the premises. Likewise, his safe exit from the premise is also to be ensured. The enquiry officer has to be extra careful in such matters. Any omission in this regard has the potential to threat the continuity of a peaceful enquiry proceeding.

■ *Enquiry Officer can grant adjournment of enquiry on reasonable grounds*

The enquiry officer can grant adjournment of enquiry at the request of the delinquent employee, or the management representative, on reasonable grounds. If at the reasonable request of the delinquent employee the enquiry officer does not grant adjournment of enquiry then the enquiry may get vitiated.

■ *Unreasonable delay in enquiry may adversely affect the theory of natural justice*

Unreasonable delay in enquiry may adversely affect the theory of natural justice. Moreover, it should also be borne in mind that a charge-sheet adversely affects the reputation of an employee. Hence, unreasonable delay in framing the charges or in conducting enquiry may mean unjustice to the employee.

In connection with a disciplinary proceeding against a government servant, there was a delay of thirteen years in framing of the charges leading to enquiry. The delay leads to the inference that the charges framed after thirteen years hold no good and it was presumed to be abandoned. It is almost impossible for the charged employee to face enquiry on a charge that was initially taken up before 13 years. *P.F. George v. State of T. Nadu & another, (1980 ILLJ 513, Madras).*

In another example a Police Constable was charge-sheeted after eighteen months for absence on one occasion and for coming late to the parade on another occasion and removed from service subsequently. Held, that the delay must be considered fatal from the point of view of reasonable opportunity to the employee to show cause against the charge levelled against him. It would be asking for the impossible to expect the employee to explain factually the reasons which occasioned the delay after eighteen months.

■ *Enquiry Officer can do local inspection*

For proper understanding of the case the enquiry officer can do local inspection. The enquiry officer can visit the site with the parties after deciding the schedule of the inspection. The local inspection is done for clarification purposes. The enquiry officer cannot base his findings on observations of local inspection. Findings must be based on evidences only. Because, observation of local inspection comes under the category of personal knowledge of the enquiry officer which cannot decide a case. Moreover, this is post occurrence of the incident. A case must be decided on evidences only.

■ *Enquiry Officer can grant personal hearing*

An enquiry officer can grant personal hearing if the rules so permit or necessitates. Personal hearing is hearing the arguments of the parties which is based on facts and evidences of the case. Personal hearing facilitates surfacing the truth of the case based on logic and counter logic provided in the arguments. The important thing is that personal hearing provides more satisfaction to the delinquent employee.

- *Enquiry Officer must maintain the confidentiality of facts deposed at the enquiry.*

Before submitting the report of the enquiry, and practically even thereafter, the enquiry officer must maintain the confidentiality of facts deposed at the enquiry. It requires lot of professional maturity to conduct an enquiry to the satisfaction of the disputing parties, specially because the enquiry officer is supposed to be an independent person. An enquiry officer should not discuss facts deposed at the enquiry in open or public forums. It can affect the future proceedings in more ways than one.

- *Copy of the enquiry proceedings must be provided to the delinquent employee*

The Enquiry Officer should maintain a daily order sheet to record in brief the business transacted on each day of the hearing. Requests and representations by either party should also be dealt with and disposed of in this sheet. Copies of the recorded order sheets will be given to the Presenting Officer and Charged Employee with their signatures thereon. Handing over the daily order sheet to the charged employee is a good practice. However, specific instruction in this regard as mentioned in the Rules and Regulations or Standing Orders of the Company must be adhered.

- *The disciplinary proceedings initiated against an employee should be according to the misconduct defined in the standing orders*

A general indiscipline unconnected with work should ordinarily not warrant a charge. Although the standing orders of many companies define misconduct as "*without prejudice to the general meaning of the term misconduct the following acts of commission or omission by an employee of the Company shall mean misconduct…*" This means whatever specifically has not been mentioned as misconduct may also be treated as so if it is subversive of discipline and lowers the image or reputation of the Company in the eyes of the people.

However, ordinarily misconduct should relate to place of work, and in relation to work. If two employees of a common employer fight away from the establishment or if any one employee assault another, outside the establishment that by itself does not become an act subversive of discipline. If such assault takes place within the premises of the employer then there may be a presumption that it affects other workmen and the question of breach of discipline may be assumed or implied.

■ A re-enquiry is possible on the same charge

In case of *Anand Narain Shukla v. State of M.P. (AIR 1979, SC 1923)*, the same possibility has been confirmed. There was an enquiry against the charged officer. He was found guilty on some of the charges levelled against him. Consequently, he was punished with reversion to the lower rank. Against this demotion order, he filed a writ in the High Court. The High Court quashed the order on the ground that the enquiry was not proper and legal. The enquiry was quashed on technical grounds. There upon the charged officer was reinstated in his original post. He was then put under suspension. A fresh proceeding was started on the basis of the same old charges. He was found guilty of some of the charges and was again reverted to a lower rank. The charged officer again filed a writ petition in the High Court challenging the fresh order of reversion. This time the High Court dismissed the petition . The charged officer then filed an appeal to the Supreme Court. The Supreme Court held that since the earlier order was quashed on technical ground, a second enquiry could be held on merits.

■ A departmental enquiry can be conducted simultaneously with prosecution in a court of law

There is no provision in law which empowers Courts to stay departmental proceedings merely because a criminal prosecution of the same person is launched in a Court of Law. These are two different enquiries. The object of departmental proceeding is to ascertain if the employee is a fit person to be retained in service and the object of the Court trial is to see if the ingredients of the offence have been made out warranting conviction. The Principles of Natural Justice require that an employer must wait for the decision at least of the trial Court before taking action against an employee. Though ordinarily a departmental action is not initiated in regard to sub-judice matter, yet there is no bar on it. *The case of Delhi Cloth and General Mills Ltd. v. Kushal Bhan (AIR 1960 SC 806)* is worth mentioning here. In the instant case, the Supreme Court observed that often employers stay enquiries pending decision of the criminal courts and that is fair. If the case is of grave nature or involves question of facts or law, which are not simple, it would be advisable for the employer to wait the decision of the trial court so that the defence of the employee in the criminal court may not be prejudiced. However, the discretion lies with the Employer.

- *If both criminal case and departmental enquiry is based on identical and same set of facts the departmental enquiry should wait*

It is advisable that when the facts for criminal case and departmental enquiry are same and identical, the departmental enquiry should wait. It is because if the charged employee is acquitted with honour by the court, an adverse finding, if it comes out to be so, will stand on a weak ground. The case of *Kusheshwar Dubey v. Bharat Coking Coal Ltd. (AIR 1988 SC 2118)* needs a mention in this regard. In the instant case, the Supreme Court observed that if the criminal trial as well as disciplinary proceedings are based upon the same set of facts, it can be very well said that imputation in the disciplinary proceedings as well as in criminal trial are similar if not identical. It was, therefore, held that the departmental proceedings are liable to be stayed.

- *If proceedings of criminal charge in court is unduly delayed, the employer can initiate, reinitiate if stayed, departmental enquiry*

The case of *State of Rajasthan v. B.K. Meena, IAS and Ors., (1996) 6 SCC 417,* needs a mention in this regard. In the instant case, the Supreme Court has made a distinction between Criminal Trial and Disciplinary Enquiry. The Apex Court held that both proceedings i.e., the Criminal Trial and Disciplinary Enquiry have different approach, objective, standard of proof, mode of enquiry and rules. In disciplinary proceedings, the question is whether the charged official is guilty of such conduct as would merit his removal from service or a less severe punishment. Whereas in criminal proceedings, the question is whether the offences alleged to have been committed by the suspect is established, and if established, what sentence should be imposed upon him. Staying of disciplinary proceedings, pending criminal proceeding should not be a matter of course, but a considered decision. Even if, stayed at one stage, the decision may require reconsideration if the criminal trial is unduly delayed.

123

- ## *Application of Article 20 (2) of Constitution: Criminal Proceeding after departmental action and vice-versa*

At times, in view of the serious nature of the allegation, it may be necessary to initiate criminal proceedings against a public servant or employee in a commercial undertaking even after his dismissal or removal from service in a departmental action. In other words, can a public servant or an employee be prosecuted on a charge of bribery or criminal misconduct after his removal from service on the same set of facts? If so, does it contravene the constitutional guarantee as contemplated by Article 20(2) of the Constitution of India which says a person cannot be punished twice for the same offence? This question was set at rest by the Supreme Court in its judgement in the case of *S.A. Venkataraman v. The State (1958 Cr.L.J. 254 SC)*. It was held that Article 20(2) refers to proceedings before a Court of law for an offence, where there is prosecution and conviction. In a departmental proceeding, there is neither any prosecution nor any conviction by a Court of Law. Therefore, a public servant who has been punished for an official misconduct in a departmental proceeding may still be subjected to a criminal prosecution if the misconduct alleged is also a criminal offence. Thus prohibition as contained in Art. 20(2) of the Constitution in such a case is inoperative.

- ## *A formal charge and enquiry is required in case of a probationer employee*

Unless confirmed on job a probationer is not a full fledged employee in strict sense of the term. A Probation is basically in trial period to prove himself suitable for the job offered to him. However, the disciplinary procedures are applicable to him in the same manner as applicable to a permanent employee of the organization. Neither a permanent employee nor a probationer can be punished without a formal charge and enquiry. But in case of probationer, a less formal enquiry may be sufficient. *Bishanlal Gupta V. State of Haryana & Others (1978 ILLJ 317 SC)*.

- ## *Employees cannot be held guilt in group: Misconduct has to be proved very particularly*

A charge-sheet has to be framed against a particular workman with very specific charges levelled against him. A charge-sheet cannot be framed for a group of workmen. *In Punjab National Bank Ltd. v.*

Workmen, (AIR 1960 ,SC 160), workmen were charged with active participation in an act of misconduct. It was held that misconduct must be proved against each workman before each of them can be held guilty. It was further held that the theory of conspiracy has no application for activities of the union which represents them.

It may be mentioned here that unlike an FIR in case of criminal proceeding a charge-sheet cannot be filed against an anonymous person or a group of persons or mob. A charge-sheet in a domestic enquiry to prove an act of misconduct against an employee has to be very particular in terms of employee to whom it is served, and very specific in terms of charges that are levelled against the employee.

■ *Admissibility of legal practitioner at the domestic enquiry for defending the delinquent employee*

This decision lies with the enquiry officer. However, the enquiry officer must exercise his judgement based on two things (a) Does the rule of the organization specifically forbids an employee to be represented by a legal practitioner at the enquiry. If it is so, it may not be possible for the enquiry officer to allow a legal practitioner for the assistance of the delinquent employee. (b) In case of Standing Orders or Service Rules being silent on this issue does it appear right to allow a legal practitioner. Based on the complexities of the case and weighing the legal competence of the presenting officer of the management the enquiry officer may take a decision in favour of the delinquent employee.

It may be mentioned that the standing orders of some organizations specifically mention that in enquiry proceedings a delinquent employee may take the assistance from a fellow co-worker or an executive committee member of the Union of the employee, but generally the Rules are silent regarding admissibility of a legal practitioner at the enquiry.

The enquiry officer should, however, allow assistance to the delinquent employee by a legal practitioner considering the nature of charges and issues which may arise in course of the enquiry. Where legally trained minds represent the employer in the domestic enquiry, and the enquiry officer is a man of employer's establishment, the weighted scales and titled balance can be partly restore if the delinquent is given the same legal assistance as the employer has employed.

In the case of *Board of Trustees for the Port of Bombay v. D.R. Nadkarni and thers (1983 ILLJ SC*, on the question of the claim of the charge-sheeted workmen to be represented by a legal practitioner, the Supreme Court held that where the employer has on its pay-roll Labour Officer, Legal Advisers and lawyers in the garb of employees and they are appointed as presenting cum prosecuting officers, the enquiry officer should, unless the rules prescribed for such enquiry place an embargo on the right of the employee to be presented by a legal practitioner, in his discretion permit the employee to appear through a legal practitioner..In *C.L. Subramaniam v. Collector of Customs, (AIR 1972 SC 2118),* the Supreme Court observed that the fact that the case against the delinquent employee was being handled by a trained prosecutor was a good ground for allowing the appellant to engage a legal practitioner to defend him lest the scales be tilted against him.

In the case of *A.J. Vaswani v. Union of India (1983, April Lab IC 625, per J. Gose & Pyne)*, the Calcutta High Court found that the appellant Sri Vaswani, a preventive officer under the collector of customs (under suspension) during the departmental enquiry prayed for representation through a lawyer but the prayer was not allowed. The department had an experienced Police inspector to present its case before the enquiry officer. No government servant agreed to represent the delinquent officer in the enquiry because top officials who were witnesses in the enquiry had to be cross-examined. There were legal and factual complexities. Further, legal issues were involved in the case. Besides, the delinquent was not fit in body and mind since long suspension had affected his health and mind. Considering all factors, the High Court held that the above facts and circumstances were good grounds justifying a permission to the delinquent to be represented by a legal practitioner.

■ *Charges of misconduct can be levelled and enquiry can proceed only against an employee who is in service*

Disciplinary procedure can be initiated against an employee while the employee is in service. What will happen then when an employee commits a serious misconduct at the close of his retirement or superannuation is a pertinent question. It may be noted that in such a case a departmental or domestic enquiry can be initiated while the delinquent employee is in service, and it can continue after the retirement or superannuation of the employee. Till that time the employer can withhold the retirement benefits that the delinquent employee is entitled to. However, disciplinary proceedings cannot be initiated when the employee is no more in service.

In the case of *M.C. Dhir v. State of Punjab*, *(1982 Oct. lab IC NOC 117) (Punjab & Haryana)* the petitioner employee of the State of Punjab was suspended pending completion of the department proceedings, but as his age of retirement came just after the suspension he was allowed to retire and so the suspension order was revoked. But, one and half years after his retirement, the case was reopened under Rule 2.2 (b) of the Punjab Civil Services (punishment & appeal rules, 1970) and a disciplinary proceeding was initiated against the retired employee. The Supreme Court held that initiation of disciplinary proceedings against the employee after his retirement was wholly without jurisdiction (1970 Lab IC 271 SC).

■ *If reasonable opportunity of being heard is evident in enquiry proceedings then minor change in procedure cannot vitiate enquiry*

The requirement that reasonable opportunity of being heard must be given has two elements. The first in that opportunity to be heard must be given; the second is that this opportunity must be reasonable.

In the case of *Motor Industries Co. Ltd. V. D Adinarayanappa and another*, *(1978, I LLJ 443 Karn)*, the issue before His Lordship was whether a domestic enquiry held by the management which is valid in all respects *is invalid on the ground that before holding the enquiry, an opportunity of answering the charges should have been given to the delinquent employee.* In the instant case it was held that informing the delinquent employee of the specific charges levelled against him in writing and giving him an opportunity to defend himself in an enquiry, fulfills the requirement of the principles of natural justice and it is not a necessary requirement of the principles of natural justice that before holding an enquiry, an earlier opportunity of furnishing reply to the charges should be given to the delinquent.

What constitutes a reasonable opportunity in a domestic or departmental enquiry has been defined by the Supreme Court in the case of Khem Chand v Union Of India (AIR, 1958 SC 300). In the case of Khem Chand v. Union of India what constitutes reasonable opportunity has been defined in the following manner-

(a) An opportunity to deny his guilt and establish his innocence which he can only do, if he is told what the charges levelled against him are and the allegations on which such charges are based

(b) An opportunity to defend himself by cross examining the witnesses produced against him and by examining himself or any other witnesses to support his defence and finality

(c) An opportunity to make his representation as to why the proposed punishment should be inflicted on him which he can do only if the competent authority, after the enquiry is over and after applying his mind to the gravity or otherwise of the charges proved against the government servant, tentatively proposes to inflict one of the three major punishments and communicates the same to the government servant.

Reasonable opportunity should be provided to a delinquent employee to enable him to defend himself against the charges levelled on him. The opportunity should be provided in all fairness.

SPECIMEN CHART SHOWING DISCIPLINARY POWERS IN ANY ORGANIZATION-I

IMPORTANT NOTE:

It may be noted that the Court may ask for proper delegation of authority in matters of disciplinary action to satisfy itself that the decision of discharge or dismissal of the employee has been taken by the competent authority.

How the disciplinary powers are delegated in an organization has been mentioned below:

(A) AUTHORIZATION OF POWERS REGARDING EMPLOYEE DISCIPLINE MATTERS TO THE MANAGING DIRECTOR BY THE BOARD OF DIRECTORS:

The Board of Directors vide resolution item no._____ dt._____ has decided to authorize the Managing Director to take all necessary actions to maintain discipline in the Company, and for this purpose he is ,hereby, authorized to take disciplinary action against any grade or designation of employee, including the punishment of discharge and dismissal, as per the procedure laid down in the rules and regulations and / or Standing Orders of the Company.

Provided, however, that for deciding a punishment of discharge or dismissal for an employee designated as General Manager or above, the Managing Director is required to take the consent of Board of Directors. The consent of two members of the Board of Directors, other than the Managing Director himself, will be taken to mean the consent of the Board.

Provided further that for administrative convenience the Managing Director may sub-delegate the powers in this regard to appropriate levels in the Company, as he may deem fit.

(SIGNED BY MEMBERS OF THE BOARD OF DIRECTORS)

SPECIMEN CHART SHOWING DISCIPLINARY POWERS IN ANY ORGANIZATION-II

(B.) POWER OF DELEGATION IN EMPLOYEE DISCIPLINE MATTERS BY THE MANAGING DIRECTOR TO SUBORDINATE AUTHORITIES:

In pursuance of the powers delegated by the Board Of Directors vide resolution item no._____dt._____ the Managing Director is, hereby, pleased to delegate the powers relating to employee discipline matters in the following manner:

The authority, thus, invested with disciplinary powers, vide this delegation of authority by the Managing Director, will take disciplinary action following the rules and regulations and / or the Standing Orders of the Company.

DESIGNATION	POWERS RELATING TO DISCIPLINARY ACTION			
	POWER TO SHOW CAUSE	POWER TO PUNISH UPTO SUSPENSION	POWER TO DISMISS & DISCHARGE	
PRESIDENT, VICE-PRESIDENT,GENERAL MANAGER	MANAGING DIRECTOR	MANAGING DIRECTOR	MANAGING DIRECTOR WITH CONSENT OF THE BOARD OF DIRECTORS	
DEPUTY GM, ASST. GM, SR. MANAGER, MANAGER	GENERAL MANAGER & ABOVE	GENERAL MANAGER & ABOVE	GENERAL MANAGER & ABOVE WITH CONSENT OF MANAGING DIRECTOR	
DEPUTY MANAGER, ASST. MANAGER, SENIOR OFFICER, OFFICER,EXECUTIVE	ASST. GM & ABOVE	ASST. GM & ABOVE	GENERAL MANAGER & ABOVE	
SUPERVISORS	MANAGER & ABOVE	MANAGER & ABOVE	GENERAL MANAGER & ABOVE	
WORKERS & STAFF	MANAGER & ABOVE	MANAGER & ABOVE	GENERAL MANAGER & ABOVE	

(SIGNED BY THE MANAGING DIRECTOR & STAMP)

SPECIMEN COPY OF A CHARGE-SHEET

Charge Sheet Reference Number:/Date:
Name of the Employee:
Personal Identification Number:/Grade:
Designation:/Department:
Address for Correspondence:
(LOCAL) (PERMANENT)

_____

_____

_____

Mr._____,
This has been reported against you that on _____
(day/date) at around_____(time) at/
near _____ (mention place) you
(mention the exact misconduct in short and substance)

_____

_____

The above act constitutes misconduct on your part and is a violation of Standing Order /Service Rule No..[mention the related rule(s) and sub- rule(s)] _____

_____Of the Company.

You are, hereby, required to furnish an explanation to the charges levelled against you within 48 hours from the service of this charge-sheet failing which it will be assumed that you have no explanation to offer. If the explanation submitted by you is found satisfactory, the charges levelled against you will be dropped and no further action will be taken. If however, the explanation submitted by you is not found satisfactory then an enquiry into the charges will be conducted by Shri_____ (Mention Name , Designation and Department) who is, hereby, appointed as the enquiry officer in this case. (Note: There can be more than one enquiry officer also)

With immediate effect, you will be under suspension pending enquiry into the charges levelled against you.(Mention only when the employee is to be kept in suspension pending enquiry)

(The below mentioned part may/may not be mentioned. Mentioning this part is not illegal or invalid. It depends on Convenience and Practice as the first notice of the enquiry date is already served along with the charge-sheet).

The enquiry into the charges will be conducted on_____   _____
(Day / Date)at_____(Time) in the office of the
_____(Mention Place) by the Enquiry Officer wherein you have to be physically present for the enquiry.

If you do not report for the enquiry at the abovementioned day, date , time and place then the enquiry will proceed ex-parte in your absence for which you alone will be responsible.

_____

(Name , Designation & Signature of Issuing Authority & Stamp)

Copy to: Employee (Local & Permanent Address) / Departmental Head (Proper Channel) / Establishment Section (For Recoding in Employee File) / Security Gate (For Entry in case of Suspension)/ Accounts Section (Prior & Proper intimation for payment of Subsistence Allowance)/Enquiry Officer.

SPECIMEN COPY OF SUSPENSION PENDING ISSUE OF A FORMAL CHARGE-SHEET

(IN RIOTOUS OR DISORDERLY BEHAVIOUR/ ACT SUBVERSIVE OF DISCIPLINE)

Charge sheet Reference Number:/Date
Name of the Employee:
Personal Identification Number/:Grade
Designation:/Department:
Mr._____,
On_____(Day/ Date)at around_____(Time) at/near
_____(Place)

Your hit your superior Mr. _____(Mention Name , Personal Number & Designation) with an iron rod several times as a result of which he has suffered serious injuries on head and other parts of the body.

The above act constitutes misconduct on your part, and is violation of Service Rule/ Standing Order No. (Mention Rule and Sub-Rule) _____of the Company .

This is a very serious act of misconduct which warrants your forthwith suspension from duty pending issue of a formal charge-sheet to you.

_____

(Name , Designation & Signature of Issuing Authority & Stamp)

Copy to: Employee / Departmental Head (Proper Channel) / Establishment Section (For Recoding in Employee File) / Security Gate (To Check Entry in case of Suspension)/ A copy to be attached with the FIR to the Police.

Note: Here the injured superior may need hospitalization , or treatment for several days. He would not be available for enquiry for some days. At the same time it is not advisable to allow such a violent employee at work. Hence it is good to keep him in suspension pending issue of a formal charge-sheet. An FIR should be lodged alongside by the management particularly because the employee may succumb to injuries, and die.

SPECIMEN COPY OF SUSPENSION PENDING ISSUE OF A FORMAL CHARGE-SHEET

(IN A THEFT CASE)

Charge sheet Reference Number:/Date
Name of the Employee:
Personal Identification Number/:Grade
Designation:/Department:
Mr._____,

You were caught red-handed on_____ (Day/Date) at around _____(Mention time) at the _____gate (Mention Place / Gate No. of Security, if any) while stealing away _____ (Mention exact description of the material and number)belonging to the Company by the security guard/s _____[Mention the name(s) & Designation].

The above act constitutes misconduct on your part, and is violation of Service Rule/ Standing Order No. (Mention Rule and Sub-Rule)_____of the Company .

This is a very serious act of misconduct which warrants your forthwith suspension from duty pending issue of a formal charge-sheet to you.

_____

(Name , Designation & Signature of Issuing Authority & Stamp)

Copy to: Employee / Departmental Head (Proper Channel) / Establishment Section (For Recoding in Employee File) / Security Gate (To Check Entry in case of Suspension)/ A copy to be attached with the FIR to the Police.

Note: An FIR should also be lodged by the management. A copy of the FIR is required for prosecution. Criminal Proceeding may proceed side by side.

SPECIMEN COPY OF A PUNISHMENT LETTER
(SUSPENSION AS PUNISHMENT)

Charge sheet Reference Number:/Date
Name of the Employee:
Personal Identification Number/:Grade
Designation:/Department:
Mr._____,

Please refer to the above charge-sheet no_____ dated_____issued to you for your alleged act of misconduct which was a violation of _____

[Mention Rule(S) and Sub-Rule(s)]of the Standing Orders/ Service Rules of the Organization.

In the enquiry conducted into the charges, the Enquiry Officer has found you guilty of the charges levelled against you. The management agrees with the findings of the enquiry officer.

For your above act of misconduct you will be suspended from duty for a period of 15 days, from _____(day & date) to_____ (day & date), both days inclusive.

You will report for duty from_____(Mention day & Date) in _____(Shift, if any). (It is essential to mentioned this part)

_____

(Name , Designation & Signature of Issuing Authority & Stamp)

134

Copy to: Employee (Local & Permanent) / Departmental Head (Proper Channel) / Establishment Section (For Recoding in Employee File) / Security Gate (To Check Entry in case of Suspension)/ Accounts Section (No payment for the period of Suspension).

SPECIMEN COPY OF A SECOND SHOW CAUSE NOTICE

(IN CASE OF EX-PARTE ENQUIRY)

Charge sheet Reference Number:/Date
Name Of The Employee:
Personal Identification Number/:Grade
Designation:/Department:
Mr._____ ,

Please refer to the charge-sheet No. _____ dated_____ issued to you for your alleged act of misconduct which was a violation of Service Rule No./Standing Order No_____ _____of the Company.

The enquiry into the above charge-sheet was conducted by the Enquiry Officer Mr._____ from _____(date) to_____(date) in which you did not cooperate, and hence the enquiry was conducted ex-parte after giving sufficient opportunity to you to participate in the enquiry.

The Enquiry Officer has found you guilty of the charges levelled against you.

The gravity of the charges levelled against you justify dismissal from service as punishment.

You are being given an opportunity vide this letter to explain your contention as to why a punishment of dismissal should not be inflicted on you.

We have attached a copy of the findings of the enquiry officer as also the proceedings of the enquiry to enable you to present your explanation. Your explanation must reach us within seven days from the date of issue of this letter. Your letter of explanation will be considered on merit.

If you do not provide any explanation within stipulated time, or, in case your explanation is not found satisfactory, the management will proceed in this matter as stated above.

_____

(Name, Designation & Signature of Punishing Authority)
Encl: As mentioned above

Copy to: Employee/ Establishment (For Records)

SPECIMEN COPY OF A DISCHARGE LETTER
(DISCHARGE AS PUNISHMENT)

Charge sheet Reference Number:/Date
Name Of The Employee:
Personal Identification Number/:Grade
Designation:/Department:
Mr._____ ,

Please refer to the charge-sheet No. _____ dated_____ issued to you for your alleged act of misconduct which was a violation of Service Rule No./Standing Order No_____ _____of the Company.

The enquiry into the above charge-sheet was conducted by the Enquiry Officer Mr._____ from _____(date) to_____(date) in which you also participated.

The Enquiry Officer found you guilty of the charges levelled against you. After careful consideration of the report of the enquiry, and findings of the enquiry officer the management held that the gravity of the charges levelled against you justify dismissal from service as punishment. An opportunity, however, was provided to you vide letter ref. No. _____dated_____ to show cause as to why a punishment of dismissal should not be inflicted on you. Your explanation to the said show cause has not been found satisfactory.

However, considering your past record the management has decided not to dismiss you, but to discharge you from the service of the Company. You will be discharged from the service of the Company with effect from _____(Day/Date).

You are, hereby, instructed to contact the accounts department of the Company on any working day during normal working hours and settle all your dues with the Company.

_____

(Name, Designation & Signature of Punishing Authority)

Copy to: Employee / Departmental Head (Proper Channel) / Establishment Section (For Recoding in Employee File) / Security Gate (To Check Entry)/ Accounts Section (For payment of Dues).

SPECIMEN COPY OF A DISMISSAL LETTER
(DISMISSAL AS PUNISHMENT)

Charge sheet Reference Number:/Date
Name of the Employee:
Personal Identification Number/:Grade
Designation:/Department:
Mr._____ ,

Please refer to the charge-sheet No. _____ dated_____issued to you for your alleged act of misconduct was a violation of Service Rule No./Standing Order No_____

_____

The enquiry into the above charge-sheet was conducted by the Enquiry Officer Mr._____ from _____(date) to_____(date) in which you also participated. The Enquiry Officer found you guilty of the charges levelled against you. After careful consideration of the report of the enquiry, and the findings of the enquiry officer, the management held that the gravity of the charges levelled against you justified your dismissal from service of the Company.

An opportunity, however, was provided to you vide letter ref. No. _____dated _____ to show cause as to why a punishment of dismissal should not be inflicted on you.

Your explanation to the said show cause has not been found satisfactory and it has been finally decided to dismiss you from the service of the Company with effect from _____ _____(day/date).

No further communication in this regard will be entertained by the management.

_____

(Name, Designation & Signature of Punishing Authority)

Copy to: Employee / Departmental Head (Proper Channel) / Establishment Section (For Recoding in EmployeeFile) / Security Gate (To Check Entry)

CHAPTER VII

REINSTATEMENT AND COMPENSATION

The word 'reinstatement' means 'to restore to a former position, status etc'. The word 'Compensation' in common parlance means 'to counterbalance or to make up for'. Reinstatement applies where an employee is wrongfully, illegally or invalidly discharged or dismissed by the employer and subsequently he is restored back in his employment along with the back wages by the Orders of the Court or Industrial Tribunal. The legal machinery of the government comes to the rescue of an aggrieved employee whose 'means of livelihood' is attacked by the employer in whimsical and arbitrary manner. On occasions, the Court or Industrial Tribunal grants compensation in lieu of reinstatement. The Industrial Relations factor, the estranged relations between the employer and the dismissed or discharged employee, and such similar situations forces the Court or Industrial Tribunal to grant compensation to a discharged or dismissed employee in lieu of reinstatement to makes up for the hardships suffered by the employee.

When a discharged or dismissed worker is reinstated in job his contract of service with the employer is deemed to be continuous. He is, therefore, entitled to wages at the rate he was given prior to his discharge or dismissal. The Industrial Tribunal or Court grants full or partial back wages depending on the merits of the case.

Reinstatement means restoration of service of a terminated employee to his original post assuming no break in contract of employment and providing his all back pay, allowance and other privileges. *Mettupalayam Coonoor Services Ltd. v. Workman, (1952) I LLJ 653 (LAT).*

The other privileges have been interpreted in various manner depending upon the peculiarity and merits of a case. In similar way, compensation is also awarded depending on peculiarity of a case. As a matter of fact, compensation is given by court in unusual or exceptional circumstances. *Hindustan Steel Ltd. v. A. K. Roy, (1969) 3 SCC 573.*

However, this has been held by the Courts on more than one occasion that for wrongful or illegal dismissal the normal rule is reinstatement with back wages.

REINSTATEMENT OF A DISCHARGED OR DISMISSED EMPLOYEE:

Reinstatement of the dismissed or discharged industrial employee may be granted primarily by Industrial Tribunal and Labour Court under section 11A of the Industrial Disputes Act. But, a civil Court, under the provisions of the Specific Relief Act, and a High Court, by writ petition under Article 226 of the Constitution, can also provide such relief of reinstatement of a discharged or dismissed employee. An employee discharged or dismissed from the service of the Government seeks redress in Civil Court, Court of Administrative Tribunal or a High Court.

When can a suit lie in which court has been briefly mentioned below for a clear understanding as to wherefrom a relief is sought and under what circumstances.

CIVIL COURT

■ If an employee seeks a declaration from the Court that the Order of dismissal or discharge is illegal and invalid, *ab initio*, then he can file a suit in Civil Court. The Court, based on the merits of the case, if observes that the order of dismissal or discharge of an employee is illegal and invalid, it declares the order of the management or the employer as legally bad and sets aside the dismissal and discharge order. As such, discharge or dismissal is considered null and void and the employee is considered in employment in continuity as if no discharge or dismissal had happened. Reinstatement of a dismissed or discharged employee naturally flows from the order of the Civil Court when it sets aside an illegal and invalid order of dismissal and discharge. Since the employee is considered in service in continuity, as the order of dismissal or discharge is considered as void, technically the term reinstatement can be considered a misnomer. The employee is also entitled to back wages for the period discharge or dismissal was in effect.

■ As a rule, Civil Court has no jurisdiction to sit in judgement against an order of government dismissing its servants. However, it can examine if the provisions of Article 311 has been observed or not. If the provisions of Article 311 are not observed and an employee is dismissed or discharged then Civil Court can interfere and set aside such order.

A reinstatement naturally results and along with it the back wages for the intervening period or discharge and dismissal.

- A right assigned to an employee by any Act or Statute of the government can be protected by Civil Court. If such right is infringed upon then remedy lies in Civil Court.

- Industrial Disputes under Section 2A of the ID Act also falls in Civil Court if the employee only seeks a declaration by the Court that his discharge or dismissal order is illegal and should be declared null and void. The employee has a choice in this regard either to approach Civil Court or Industrial Tribunal. *Sukh Ram V. State of Haryana, (1982) I SLR 633.*

- The Civil Court grants relief under the provisions of the Specific Relief Act.

Sri Mulla has described circumstances in which the jurisdiction of Civil Court is taken away in respect of matters entrusted to a special tribunal-

- When the statute re-enacts a right existing at common law and provides a special form of remedy therefor, the jurisdiction of the Civil Court to deal with the matter is not excluded unless the statute says so expressly or by necessary implications.

- Where the statute creates a new right but provides no special remedy therefore, it can be enforced in the Ordinary Civil Court.

- Where a statute creates a new right not existing at common law and specifies a particular mode in which it is to be enforced, it bars by implication the jurisdiction of Civil Courts.

- Where the jurisdiction of the Civil Court is excluded still they would have jurisdiction to examine into cases where the provision of the statute have not been complied with or where the statutory tribunal has not acted in conformity with the fundamental principles of judicial procedure, or natural justice. (*Code of Civil Procedure, Vol. I, p.40)*

The Supreme Court in the case of *Premier Automobiles Ltd. v. Kamlakar Shantaram Wadke, (1976) I SCC 496,* has laid down that Civil Courts can interfere in industrial matters in following situations-

- If the dispute is not an industrial dispute, nor does it relate to enforcement of any other right under the Act, the remedy lies only in Civil Court.

■ If the dispute is an industrial dispute arising out of a right or liability under the general or common law and not under the Act, the jurisdiction of civil court is alternative. It is upon the suitor to choose a remedy either by Civil Court or by Industrial Tribunal or Labour Court.

Territorial Jurisdiction of a Civil Court

■ Territorial Jurisdiction of a Civil Court lies under whose jurisdiction the cause of action arises either completely or in part and/or where the defendant resides.

LABOUR COURT AND INDUSTRIAL TRIBUNAL

■ A dispute relating to specific terms of employment can lie only in Labour Court or Industrial Tribunal under the Industrial Disputes Act. Section 11-A of the Industrial Disputes Act assigns wide powers to the Labour Courts and Tribunals in matters of discharge and dismissal of an employee by the employer.

■ The Labour Court and Industrial Tribunal can not only set aside the order of dismissal or discharge but can change the quantum of punishment given to an employee by the management. The Labour Court and Industrial Tribunals have appellate powers. They can go into the details of the enquiry conducted by the management.

■ The Industrial Tribunals have been invested with more powers in this regard. It can mitigate the punishment given to an employee. The Industrial Tribunal can change the order of dismissal into discharge. It can set aside the order of dismissal and discharge, and can award a lesser punishment befitting the gravity of misconduct, considering the tenure of service left of an employee, his past record, his conduct during the enquiry proceeding and his attitude towards the employer.

■ If an employee challenges the order of dismissal or discharge passed by the management then he raises an industrial dispute and approaches the government for relief. The Government makes a reference to the Labour Court or Industrial tribunal to provide specific relief as mentioned in the reference made by the Government. Along with the specific relief, such as setting aside of the order of discharge or dismissal the Industrial Tribunal or Labour Court also provides the relief of appropriate back wages with allowances and privileges.

The Supreme Court in the case of *Premier Automobiles Ltd. v. Kamlakar Shantaram Wadke,(1976) I SCC 496,* has laid down that Labour Courts and Industrial Tribunal can interfere in industrial matters in following situations-

- If the Industrial dispute relates to the enforcement of a right or an obligation created under the ID Act, then the only remedy available to a suitor lies in Industrial Tribunal or Labour Court.
- If the right which is sought to be enforced is a specific right created under the ID Act, such as chapter V-A, then the remedy for its enforcement is either section 33- C, or the raising of an industrial dispute as the case may be.

Territorial Jurisdiction of Labour Court or Industrial Tribunal

- Territorial Jurisdiction of a Labour Court or Industrial Tribunal lies as is specified or where the cause of action takes place.

HIGH COURT

- In Writ petition under Article 226 of the Constitution a High Court can interfere to provide relief to an employee against arbitrary orders of the management or that of government.
- Under Article 311 of the Constitution of India the government servants have got a protection under arbitrary act of the government. On violation of the provisions of Article 311 a government employee can seek a remedy by filing a writ petition in High Court. It may be mentioned that a government servant can directly approach the court without exhausting remedies available in department. If the matter is serious and requires immediate intervention by the court, the court does not turn down the petition.
- Protection under Article 311 is not available to employees working in private organizations. Relief is available to them under the provisions of the Fundamental Rights. The interpretation of different fundamental rights like, Right to Equality (Article 14), Equality of Opportunity in matters of Public Employment (Article 16), and Right to Life (Article 21) prepares the ground for writ petition in High Court by employees engaged in private employment.

In the case of *Sardar Bahadur v. Union of India, (1966) 2 DLT 274,* it has been mentioned that the High Court will interfere with the discharge order if it is-

(a) arbitrary, capricious and abuse of discretion or otherwise not in accordance with law
(b) contrary to constitutional right, power, privilege or immunity
(c) in excess of statutory jurisdiction, authority or determination or of statutory Rights
(d) without observance of procedure required by law
(e) unsupported by any evidence

Territorial Jurisdiction of High Court

■ Territorial Jurisdiction of High Court generally lies where the cause of action has taken place or where the order of dismissal has been communicated.

PAYMENT OF BACK WAGES AND COMPENSATION :
BACK WAGES :

Ordinarily reinstatement assumes payment of back wages to the employee. When an employee is reinstated, it implies two things. First, the contract of employment between the employee and the employer is restored or refurbished. Second, the employee becomes entitled to the same wages which he was ordinarily getting prior to his dismissal or discharge.

A reinstated employee is entitled to all back pay, allowances and other privileges which he was entitled to prior to dismissal. It is because a wrong dismissal severs the contract of employment for no fault on the part of the employee. An employee suffers mental agony, harassment and financial loss when he is rendered jobless by an act of illegal or wrong dismissal. A reinstatement heals up the wounds of the employee and freshens the contract of employment. It treats the employee as if he was continuously on job. As such, he becomes entitled to all monetary losses. It may be mentioned that the tribunal or court orders a reinstatement only when the relationship between the employee and the employer does not reach a stage from where a renovation of the contract of employment is not possible. A reinstatement, barring exceptions, also implies that the employee has not lost the confidence of the employer, and the reinstatement will not create any ugly situation in the field of industrial relations.

Normally, the tribunal or court orders full back wages at the time of reinstatement. However, depending on the circumstances partial back wages is also allowed. A curtailment in back wages is done when the discharged or dismissed employee accepts other employment during the period of discharge or dismissal. Since a dismissed or discharged employee would hardly get an employment which would offer him the same wages which he was earning prior to dismissal or discharge, a loss of earning is contemplated. By granting partial back wages the tribunal or court follows equitable formula whereby the employee makes up for the loss of wage during the period of discharge and dismissal, and the employer also has to pay part of the total back wages.

It was observed by the Court in a case that by taking up services elsewhere the employee does not lose his right to agitate the propriety of his discharge, it affects the amount of compensation. *New Victoria Mills Co. Ltd. Kanpur V. Shri Kamaludin (1952) I LLJ 179 (LAT).*

When the court had the positive evidence that the dismissed workmen had not accepted employment elsewhere during the period of discharge or dismissal they were granted full wages for the period of forced unemployment. *Kanpur Samachar Patra Karamchari Union V. Vishwamitter Press 1952 LAC 139.*

The effort of Industrial Tribunal or Court is always to promote industrial harmony and strike a balance between the rights of the employer and the employee. An employee may also be reinstated without back wages. The function of the industrial tribunal or the Labour Court constituted under the Industrial Disputes Act is not to punish an employer for the lapses, inordinate or ordinate.

A direction for withholding payment of back wages either fully or partly is considered penal in nature. It implies that penalty has been imposed on account of some fault in the workman.

There is no set rule as to what would be considered in back wages but depending on the various case laws it can be summarized in the following manner-

- Basic scale of Pay
- Dearness Allowance
- All other allowances
- Grade benefit
- Bonus
- Credit of Leave (Not Leave encashment)

If the employee gets the above benefits he is ordinarily considered to be in job without any discontinuity. Although, the Courts have granted back wages more than what has been mentioned above; which included even production incentives. But, such cases were exception.

IMPLICATION OF SECTION 17 B OF ID ACT:

Section 17 B has been inserted in the Industrial Disputes Act by Act 46 of 1982 which came into force from 21st August, 1984. The purpose of section 17 B is to provide relief to the workmen on account of pendency of disputes in higher courts.

Section17 B provides that where in any case, Labour Court, Tribunal or National Tribunal by its award directs reinstatement of any workman and the employer prefers any proceedings against such award in a High Court or Supreme Court the employee shall be liable to pay such workman, during the period of pendency of such proceedings in the High Court or Supreme Court, full wages last drawn by him, inclusive of any maintenance allowance admissible to him under any rule if the workman had not been employed in any establishment during such period and an affidavit by such workman had been filed to that effect in such court.

Provided, however, that where it is proved to the satisfaction of the High Court or the Supreme Court that such workman had been employed and had been receiving adequate remuneration during any such period or part thereof, the Court shall order that no wages shall be payable under this section for such period or part as the case may be.

The implication of Section 17 B is that the employer cannot harass the dismissed or discharged employee by dragging him into a long legal battle.

COMPENSATION:

The case of granting compensation is little bit different. Grant of Compensation is not a rule, but an exception. When an employee is wrongfully discharged or dismissed as a general rule he is to be reinstated back in job. But, when contingent upon the situation his reinstatement is not possible then he is granted compensation by the employer. It must be borne in mind that compensation for loss of employment by illegal or unjustified termination carries two reliefs for the employee - one is for reinstatement and another is for back wages.

The labour court or the tribunal has the discretion to award compensation as a substitute for reinstatement specially in cases which are unusual or exceptional where reinstatement is not advisable both in the interest of the employee as well as the employer. In such cases, reinstatement is considered inexpedient or improper. *Hindustan Steels Ltd. Rourkela v. A. K. Roy (1969) 3 SCC 513.*

Section 11 A of the Industrial Disputes Act has given wide powers to the Industrial Tribunal and Labour Court to award relief to an employee according to circumstances.

A fine example is the case of Jivan Singh v. Union Territory of Delhi. The petitioner employee was out of service for nearly sixteen years because of a bad enquiry and it was considered not prudent to reinstate him on job for physical reasons as also he was approaching his superannuation age. He was out of job for sixteen years and he had not completed minimum qualifying service of twenty years to become eligible for pension. It was directed that he should be treated as if he had rendered qualifying service for pension, and pension to be calculated on the basis that twenty years passed on the date of order, and such monthly pension should be paid to him from the date of dismissal. *Jivan Singh v. Administrator, Union Territory of Delhi, 1985 (I) SLJ 100.*

Reinstatement cannot be ordered mechanically by the Industrial Tribunal. If the Industrial Tribunal does so the order is not justified. *Assam Oil Corporation Ltd. v. Workmen, AIR 1960,SC 1264.*

If the Court considers that reinstatement would produce disharmony in the concern, it may only award compensation. The amount of such award would depend upon the circumstances of each case. *Narayan Bhanoo v. Bombay Dyeing & Mfg. Co. Ltd., 1957 ICR 964 (IC).*

It has been mentioned by the Law courts on many occasions that that it is not possible to lay down any rule or law regarding compensation relief to be provided to an employee and the matter must necessarily depend on the facts of each case from the point of view of both the employer and the employee. However, it appears that as a general rule the court considers the following points before awarding compensation relief to an employee-

■ Merits of the case of dismissal
■ Nature of alleged lapse on the part of the employee
■ Relationship between the employer and the employee

- The attitude and exhibited behaviour of the employee towards employer
- Impact of industrial relations if reinstatement is allowed
- Terms and conditions of employment
- The age of the employee
- Number of years of service put in, and remaining or left
- The possibility of termination of employment by resignation
- The burden of compensation on the employer, etc.

Merits of the case of dismissal and the nature of lapse on the part of an employee play an important role here.

RE-ENQUIRY AFTER REINSTATEMENT :

It may be mentioned that the clock does not stop after the reinstatement of an employee is ordered by the Court or Industrial Tribunal. An employer may choose to initiate a fresh enquiry against an employee on the same grounds after his reinstatement by the Orders of the Law Courts. The employer thereby escapes the default of not implementing the orders of the Court, and at the same time proceeds further to punish the employee who gets a reinstatement benefit mainly because of some technical errors in the disciplinary action.

Where an order passed in an enquiry is quashed by a Civil Court wherein the merits of the charge were not investigated then it does not bar a second enquiry into the charge. The binding effect of a judgment depends not upon any technical considerations of form but of substance. *Devendra Pratap Narain Rai Sharma v. State of U.P. (1962) I LLJ 266: AIR 1962 SC.*

However, even if the dismissal order is set aside on a technical point, the Labour Court or Industrial Tribunal can issue directions in view of the circumstances of a particular case that no second enquiry should be held. *Kasinath Deoji Shinde v. Manager Lokmanya Mills Ltd. 1951 ICR 1650 (IC).*

In case where an order is vacated only on technical grounds and not on merits of the case a second enquiry on merit can be held. It is not barred by reinstatement subsequent to the quashing of the order of dismissal on technical grounds. *Anand Narain Shukla v. State of M.P., (1980) I SCC 252.*

The very basic and important point which must be considered is that an industry runs on the basis of close co-operation between the employer and the employees and when there is harmony between them. An employee must try to earn the goodwill and confidence of the employer. An honest, hard working and well trained employee is always an asset for the employer. It is duty of an employee to best serve the interests of his master. On the other hand, an employer is supposed to protect the livelihood and interests of its employees. Any unfair labour practice, wrong administrative action or victimization tendency of the employer is bound to be resisted by the employees for very obvious reasons.

Both, the employer and the employees must remember that law always comes to the rescue of the genuinely aggrieved party. Abiding by the law is the best way to avoid the intervention by the law, which is often painful.

CHAPTER VIII

PROVISIONS OF ACTS APPLICABLE TO DOMESTIC ENQUIRY

INDUSTRIAL EMPLOYMENT (STANDING ORDERS) ACT,1946

INDUSTRIAL DISPUTES ACT, 1947

PUBLIC SERVICES (INQUIRIES) ACT,1850

Provisions of some of the statutes are directly related to the domestic enquiry. The Industrial Employment (Standing Orders) Act, 1946 and The Industrial Disputes Act, 1947 are two such statutes wherein some of the provisions relate very directly to the process of domestic enquiry. The Public Services (Inquiries) Act, 1850 is also related to the domestic or departmental enquiries.

The Industrial Employment (Standing Orders) Act, 1946 provides that every industrial establishment shall make rules relating to conditions of employment of workmen in that establishment. These rules will also contain the provisions relating to termination of employment, acts or omissions which constitute misconduct and suspension or dismissal for misconduct. The industrial establishments are also required to make rules relating to the procedure by which action against a delinquent employee will be taken by the management or the employer.

The Industrial disputes Act,1947 contains provisions like dismissal of individual workman to be considered as industrial dispute, the dispute resolution mechanism like the authority and powers of the Labour Court and Industrial Tribunal in dealing with the cases of termination, retrenchment, discharge and dismissal of workmen and conditions of service for change for which permission is to be taken by the employer from the authorities under the Act, specially before initiating any disciplinary procedure against them, are subjects linked to disciplinary enquiries.

The Public Services (Inquiries) Act, 1850 is grossly linked to the subject of departmental or domestic enquiries.

Since in this book we are concerned with the subject matter of domestic enquiry only, therefore, we will refer to only those provisions of the Act which are directly related to the subject in consideration.

INDUSTRIAL EMPLOYMENT (STANDING ORDERS) ACT, 1946

The Standing Orders lay down statutory terms and conditions of service. The certified standing orders have the force of law because it is framed as per the provisions of an statute. It is not a voluntary act on the part of an employer. It is a requirement under the law, the violation of which is subject to penalty. The Industrial Employment (Standing Orders) Act makes it mandatory for the industrial establishments to frame standing orders laying down the terms and conditions of service of the workman. The standing orders Act also provides that till the time the standing orders of a Company is duly certified under the Act, the provisions of the Model Standing Orders mentioned in the Rules under provisions of the Act will be applicable to that establishment. This means that at no time the employer is allowed to take any arbitrary action against the workman.

The Standing Orders present a statutory contract of service between the employer and the workman employed in that establishment. *Benares Electric Light & Power Co. Ltd. v. Hanuman Singh,(1972) 2 LLJ 19 (SC).*

The employer and the workman cannot enter into any contract of service inconsistent or in violation of the provisions of the Standing Orders. *Rohtak and Hissar Distt. Electric Supply Co. v. State, AIR 1966 SC 1471.*

The terms and conditions of service under the Standing Orders is once certified by the parties, i.e., the employer and the workmen, then it becomes binding on the parties. Any decision taken in good faith by the employer following the provisions of the standing orders cannot be invalidated by the industrial tribunal or labour court. For example, when the standing order provides that there will be automatic termination of service of workman in certain conditions, and if a workman is terminated on that basis then the tribunal or labour court cannot invalidate that decision of the employer provided that action was not taken by the employer as colourable exercise of the powers of the employer.

It is clear, therefore, that the provision of the Standing Orders Act are directly related to the domestic enquiry. The specific provisions of the Act have been mentioned below with relevant comments thereon.

THE SCHEDULE APPENDED TO THE ACT

The schedule appended to the Act contains provisions or matters which must be covered under the standing orders of an industrial establishment. The schedule has reference to section 2(g) and 3(2) of the Act. Matters to be provided in Standing Orders under the Act are following :

- Classification of workmen, e.g., whether permanent, temporary, apprentices, probationers or *badlis*.
- Manner of intimating to workmen periods and hours of work, holidays, paydays and wage rates.
- Shift Working
- Attendance and late coming
- Conditions of procedure in applying for, and the authority which may grant leave and holidays.
- Requirement to enter premises by certain gates, and liability to search.
- Closing and reopening of sections of the industrial establishment, and temporary stoppages of work and the rights and liabilities of the employer and workmen arising there from.
- Termination of employment, and the notice thereof to be given by the employer and workmen
- Suspension or dismissal for misconduct, and acts or omissions which constitute misconduct
- Means of redress for workmen against unfair treatment or wrongful exactions by the employer or his agents or servants.
- Any other matter which may be prescribed.

Practically, all the points of contact between the employer and the workman have the potential to raise an industrial dispute. It is, therefore, detailed rules and regulations should be contained in the Standing Orders so that both the parties are clear about how the activities in the establishment will be carried out; without leaving any scope for friction and dispute.

The standing orders also necessarily mention what would constitute a misconduct and how the punishment will be awarded by the employee. If detailed domestic enquiry procedure is not specifically mentioned then it is presumed that it would follow the theories of natural justice. Even the domestic enquiry procedure, if it is properly laid down it cannot be against the spirit of the theories of natural justice.

The standing orders necessarily contains provisions relating to termination of employment, and the notice thereof to be given by the employer and workmen. Besides, suspension or dismissal for misconduct, and acts or omissions which constitute misconduct are always mentioned in the Standing Orders. It brings some orderliness in the system.

INTERPRETATION OF STANDING ORDERS

The standing Orders also contains specific direction that how the standing orders will be interpreted in view of any confusion or controversy relating to application of the provisions of the Standing Orders. Section 13 A of the Act mentions that If any question arises as to the application or interpretation of a standing order certified under this Act, any employer or workman or a trade union or other representative body of the workmen may refer the question to any one of the Labour Courts constituted under the Industrial Disputes Act, 1947 (14 of 1947), and specified for the disposal of such proceedings by the appropriate government by notification in the Official Gazette, and the Labour Court to which the question is so referred shall, after giving the parties an opportunity of being heard, decide the question and such decision shall be final and binding on the parties.

APPLICATION OF STANDING ORDERS

The standing Orders clearly contains where the Act shall not apply. Section 13 B of the Act mentions that nothing in this Act shall apply to an industrial establishment in so far as the workmen employed therein are persons to whom the Fundamental and Supplementary Rules, Civil Services (Temporary Services) Rules, Revised Leave Rules, Civil Services Regulations, Civilians in Defence Service (Classification, Control and Appeal) Rules or the Indian Railway Establishment Code or any other rules or regulations that may be notified in this behalf by the appropriate Government in the Official Gazette, apply.

In organizations wholly or partly under the control of the Government, Central or state, separate rules and regulations may be prescribed by the government. Separate Code may also be prescribed for corporation framed by an act of the parliament, or other statutory bodies. However, one point is definite that where the Standing Orders Act do not apply it is substituted by some other Code or Rule applicable to those organizations.

PAYMENT OF SUBSISTENCE ALLOWANCE

It is specifically provided in the Standing Orders Act that during the period of suspension a workman is liable to get subsistence allowance by the employer. Section 10 A of the Act contains the provision in detail. It mentions that where any workman is suspended by the employer pending investigation or enquiry into complaints or charges of misconduct against him, the employer shall pay to such workman subsistence allowance-

■ At the rate of fifty percent of the wages which the workman was entitled to immediately preceding the date of such suspension, for the first ninety days of suspension, and

■ At the rate of seventy five percent of such wages for the remaining period of suspension if the delay in the completion of disciplinary proceedings against such workman is not directly attributed to the conduct of such workman.

It is further mentioned that if any dispute arises regarding the subsistence allowance payable to a workman then the workman or the employer concerned may refer the dispute to the Labour Court, constituted under the Industrial Disputes Act, 1947 (14 of 1947), within the local limits of whose jurisdiction the industrial establishment wherein such workman is employed is situate and the Labour Court to which the dispute is so referred shall, after giving the parties an opportunity of being heard, decide the dispute and such decision shall be final and binding on the parties.

It is mentioned that notwithstanding anything contained in the provisions of Section 10 A, where provisions relating to payment of subsistence allowance under any other law for the time being in force in any State are more beneficial than the provisions of this section, the provisions of such other law shall be applicable to the payment of subsistence allowance in that state.

The payment of subsistence allowance is compulsory because in the absence of a subsistence allowance a suspended workman will not be able to sustain his fight against his employer for the protection of his rights granted by the statutes.

TEMPORARY APPLICATION OF MODEL STANDING ORDERS

Section 12A of the Industrial Employment (Standing Orders) Act, 1946 mentions that till the time a certified standing orders of the Company comes into operation, the prescribed model standing orders framed under the Rules of the Act shall be deemed to be adopted in that establishment, and the provisions of the model standing orders shall apply to that establishment.

The provisions of the Model Standing Orders framed under the Rules of the Act has been mentioned below.

INDUSTRIAL EMPLOYMENT (STANDING ORDERS) CENTRAL RULES, 1946
Notification No. L.R. 11 (37), date the 18th December, 1946

In exercise of the powers conferred by Section 15, read with clause (b) of Section 2 of the Industrial employment (Standing Orders) Act, 1946 (XX of 1946), the Central Government is pleased to make the following rules, the same having been previously published as required by sub-section (1) of the said Section 15, namely :

1. (1) These rules may be called the Industrial Employment (Standing Orders) Central Rules, 1946,

(2) They extend to all Union territories, and shall also apply in any State (other than a Union territory) to industrial establishments under the control of the Central Government or a Railway administration or in a major port, mine or oilfield.

2. In these rules, unless there is anything repugnant in the subject or context :

(a) 'Act' means the Industrial Employment (standing Orders) Act, 1946 (XX of 1946);

(b) 'Form' means a form set out in Schedule II appended to these rules.

2-A. In the Schedule to the Act, after Item 10, the following additional matters which shall be applicable to industrial establishments in coal mines only, shall be *inserted,* namely :-

10-A. Additional matters to be provided in Standing Orders relating to industrial establishments in coal mines :-

(1) Medical aid in case of accident.

(2) Railway travel facilities.

(3) Method of filling vacancies.

(4) Transfers.

(5) Liability of manager of the establishment or mine.

(6) Service certificate.

(7) Exhibition and supply of Standing Orders.

3. (1) Save as other wise provided in sub-rule (2), the Model Standing Orders for the purposes of the Act shall be those set out in Schedule I appended to these rules.

(2) The Model Standing Orders for the purposes of the Act in respect of industrial establishment in coal mines shall be those set out in Schedule I- A appended to these rules.

4. An application for certification of standing orders shall be made in Form I.

5. The prescribed particulars of workmen for purposes of sub-section (3) of Section 3 of the Act shall be-

(1) total number employed,

(2) number of permanent workmen,

(3) number of temporary workmen,

(3-A) number of casual Workmen,

(4) number of *badlis* or substitutes,

(5) number of probationers,

(6) number of apprentices,

(7) name of the trade union, or trade unions, if any, to which the workmen belong,

(8) remarks.

6. As soon as may be after he receives an application under Rule 4 in respect of an industrial establishment, the Certifying Officer shall-

(a) Where there is a trade union of the workmen, forward a copy of the draft standing orders to the trade union together with a notice in Form II;

(b) where there is no such trade union, call a meeting of the workmen to elect three representatives, to whom he shall, upon their election, forward a copy of the draft standing orders together with a notice in Form II.

7. Standing orders certified in pursuance of sub-section (3) of Section 5 or sub-section (2) of Section 6 of the Act shall be authenticated by the signature and seal of office of the Certifying Officer or the appellate authority as the case may be, and shall be forwarded by such officer or authority within a week of authentication by registered letter post to the employer and to the trade union, or, as the case may be, the representatives of the workmen elected in pursuance of Rule. 6.

7-A. (1) Any person desiring to prefer an appeal in pursuance of sub-section (1) of Section 6 of the Act shall draw up a memorandum of appeal setting out the grounds of appeal and forward it in quintuplicate to the appellate authority accompanied by a certified copy of the standing orders, amendments or modifications, as the case may be.

(2) The appellate authority shall, after giving the appellant an opportunity of being heard, confirm the standing orders, amendments or modifications as certified by the Certifying Officer unless it considers that there are reasons for giving the other parties to the proceedings a hearing before a final decision is made in the appeal.

(3) Where the appellate authority does not confirm the standing orders, amendments or modifications it shall fix a date for the hearing or the appeal and direct notice thereof to be given—

(a) where the appeal is filed by the employer or a workman, to trade unions of the workmen of the industrial establishments, and where there are no such trade unions to the representatives of workmen elected under clause (b) of Rule 6, or as the case may be, to the employer ;

(b) where the appeal is filed by a trade union, to the employer and all other trade unions of the workmen of the industrial establishment ;

(c) where the appeal is filed by the representatives of the workmen, to the employer and any other workmen whom the appellate authority joins as a party to the appeal.

(4) The appellant shall furnish each of the respondents with a copy of the memorandum of appeal.

(5) The appellate authority may at any stage call for any evidence it considers necessary for the disposal of the appeal.

(6) On the date fixed under sub-rule (3) for the hearing of the appeal, the appellate authority shall take such evidence as it may have called for or consider to be relevant.

8. The register required to be maintained by Section 8 of the Act shall be in Form III and shall be properly bound, and the Certifying

Officer shall furnish a copy of standing orders approved for an industrial establishment to any person applying there for on payment calculated at all following rates per copy-

(i) for the first two hundred words or less, seventy-five paisa ;

(ii) for every additional one hundred words or fraction thereof, thirty-seven paisa :

Provided that, where the said standing orders exceeds five pages, the approximate number of words per page shall be taken as the basis for calculating the total number of words to the nearest hundred, for the purpose of assessing the copying fee.

SCHEDULE I

[MODEL STANDING ORDERS IN RESPECT OF
INDUSTRIAL ESTABLISHMENTS NOT BEING
INDUSTRIAL ESTABLISHMENTS IN COAL MINES]

1. These orders shall come into force on.............

2. Classification of workmen.--(a) Workmen shall be classified as --

(1) permanent,

(2) Probationers,

(3) *badlis,*

(4) temporary,

(5) casual,

(6) apprentices.

(b) A "permanent workman" is a workman who has been engaged on a permanent basis and includes any person who has satisfactorily completed a probationary period of three months in the same or another occupation in the industrial establishment, including breaks due to sickness, accident, leave, lock-out, strike (not being an illegal strike) or involuntary closure of the establishment.

(c) A "probationer" is a workman who is provisionally employed to fill a permanent vacancy in a post and has not completed three months' service therein. If a permanent employee is employed as a probationer in a new post he may, at any time during the probationary period of three months, be reverted to his old permanent post.

(d) A *"badli"* is a workman who is appointed in the post of a permanent workman or probationer who is temporarily absent.

(e) A "temporary workman" is a workman who has been engaged for work which is of an essentially temporary nature likely to be finished within a limited period.

(f) A "casual workman" is a workman whose employment is of a casual nature.

(g) An "apprentice" is a learner who is paid an allowance during the period of his training.

3. Tickets.--(1) Every workman shall be given a permanent ticket unless he is a probationer, *badli, temporary worker or apprentice.*

(2) Every permanent workman shall be provided with a departmental ticket showing his number, and shall, on being required to do so, show it to any person authorized by the manager to inspect it.

(3) Every *badli* shall be provided with the *badli* card on which shall be entered the days on which he has worked in the establishment, and which shall be surrendered if he obtains permanent employment.

(4) Every temporary workman shall be provided with a 'temporary' ticket which he shall surrender on his discharge.

(5) Every casual worker shall be provided with a "casual" card, on which shall be entered the days on which he has worked in the establishment.

(6) Every apprentice shall be provided with an 'apprentice' card, which shall be surrendered if he obtains permanent employment.

4. Publication of working time.--The periods and hours of work for all classes of workers in each shift shall be exhibited in English and in the principal languages of workman employed in the establishment on notice-boards maintained at or near the main entrance of the establishment and at the time-keeper's office, if any.

5. Publication of holidays and pay-days.—Notices specifying (a) the days observed by the establishment as holidays, and (b) pay-days shall be pasted on the said notice-boards.

6. Publication of wage rates.—Notices' specifying the rates of wages payable to all classes of workman and for all classes of work shall be displayed on the said notice-boards.

7. Shift working.--More than one shift may be worked in a department or departments or any section of a department of the establishment at the discretion of the employer. If more than one shift is worked, the workmen shall be liable to be transferred from one shift to another. No shift working shall be discontinued without two months' notice being given in writing to the workmen prior to such discontinuance; provided that no such notice shall be necessary if the closing of the shift is under agreement with the workmen affected. If as a result of the discontinuance of the shift working, any workmen are to be retrenched, such retrenchment shall be effected, in accordance with the provisions of the Industrial Disputes Act, 1947 (14 of 1947), and the rules made there under. If shift working is restarted, the workmen shall be given notice and re-employed in accordance with the provisions of the said Act and the said rules.

7-A. Notice of changes in shift working.--Any notice of discontinuance or of re-starting of a shift working required by Standing Order 7 shall be in the form appended to these orders and shall be served in the following manner, namely :

The notice shall be displayed conspicuously by the employer on a notice-board at the main entrance to the establishment [*****] :

Provided that where any registered trade union of workmen exists, a copy of the notice shall also be served by registered post on the Secretary of such union.

8. Attendance and late coming.--All workmen shall be at work at the time fixed and notified under Paragraph 4. Workmen attending late will be liable to the deductions provided for in the Payment of Wages Act, 1936.

NOTE.- All workmen shall have to do the work in establishment at the time fixed and notified under Para 4. There is a provision for deduction in the payment if some one becomes late according to the Payment of Wages Act. 1936.

9. Leave.--(1) Holidays with pay will be allowed as provided for in Chapter VIII of the Factories Act, 1948 and other holidays in accordance with law, contract, custom and usage.

(2) A workman who desires to obtain leave of absence shall apply to the employer or any other officer of the industrial establishment specified in this behalf by the employer, who shall issue orders on the application within a week of its submission or two days prior to the commencement of the leave applied for, whichever is earlier, provided that if the leave applied for is to commence on the date of the application or within three days thereof, the order shall be given on the same day. If the leave asked for is granted a leave pass shall be issued to the worker. If the leave is refused or postponed, the fact of such refusal or postponement and the reasons there for shall be recorded in writing in a register to be maintained for the purpose, and if the worker so desires, a copy of the entry in the register shall be supplied to him. If the workman after proceeding on leave desires

an extension thereof he shall apply to the employer or the officer specified in this behalf by the employer] who shall send a written reply either granting or refusing extension of leave to the workman if his address is available and if such reply is likely to reach him before the expiry of the leave originally granted to him.

(3)If the workman remains absent beyond the period of leave originally granted or subsequently extended, he shall lose his lien on his appointment unless he (a) returns within 8 days of the expiry of the leave and (b) explains to the satisfaction of the employer or the officer specified in this behalf by the employer], his inability to return before the expiry of his leave. In case the workman loses his lien on his appointment, he shall been titled to be kept on the *badly* list.

10. Casual leave.--A workman may be granted casual leave of absence with or without pay not exceeding 10 days in the aggregate in a calendar year. Such leave shall not be for more than three days at a time except in case of sickness. Such leave is intended to meet special circumstances which cannot be foreseen. Ordinarily, the previous permission of the head of the department in the establishment shall be obtained before such leave is taken, but when this is not possible, the head of the department shall, as soon as may be practicable, be informed in writing of the absence from and of the probable duration of such absence.

11. Payment of wages.--(1) Any wages, due to the workmen but not paid on the usual pay day on account of their being unclaimed, shall be paid by the employer on an unclaimed wage pay day in each week, which shall be notified on the notice-boards as aforesaid.

(2) All workmen will be paid wages on a working day before the expiry of the seventh or the tenth day after the last day of the wage period in respect of which the wages are payable, according as the total number of workmen employed in the establishment does not or does exceed one thousand.

12. Stoppage of work.--(1) The employer may, at any time, in the event of fire, catastrophe, breakdown of machinery or stoppage of power-supply, epidemics, civil commotion or other cause beyond his control, stop any section or sections of the establishment, wholly or partially for any period or periods without notice.

(2) In the event of such stoppage during working hours, the workmen affected shall be notified by notices put upon the notice-

board in the department concerned, and at the office of the employer and at the time-keeper's office, if any, as soon as practicable, when work will be resumed and whether they are to remain or leave their place of work. The workmen shall not ordinarily be required to remain for more than two hours after the commencement of the stoppage. If the period of detention does not exceed one hour the workmen so detained shall not be paid for the period of detention. If the period of detention exceeds one hour, the workmen so detained shall be entitled to receive wages for the whole of the time during which they are detained as a result of the stoppage. In the case of piece-rate workers, the average daily earning for the previous month shall be taken to be the daily wage. No other compensation will be admissible in case of such stoppage. Whenever practicable, reasonable notice shall be given of resumption of normal work.

(3) In case where workmen are laid off for short periods on account of failure of plant or a temporary curtailment of production, the period of unemployment shall be treated as compulsory leave either with or without pay, as the case may be. When, however, workmen have to be laid off for an indefinitely long period, their services may be terminated after giving them due notice or pay in lieu thereof.

(4) The employer may in the event of a strike affecting either wholly or partially any section or department of the establishment close down either wholly or partially such section or department and any other section or department affected by such closing down. The fact of such closure shall be notified by notices put on the notice-board in the section or department concerned and in the time-keeper's office, if any, as soon as practicable. The workmen concerned shall also be notified by a general notice, prior to resumption of work, as to when work will be resumed.

13. Termination of employment.--(1) For terminating employment of a permanent workmen, notice in writing shall be given either by the employer or the workmen - one month's notice in the case of monthly-rated workmen and two weeks' notice in the case of other workmen: one month's or two week's pay, as the case may be, may be paid in lieu of notice.

(2) No temporary workman whether monthly-rated, weekly-rated or piece-rated and no probationer or *badli* shall be entitled to any notice or pay in lieu thereof if his services are terminated, but

the services of a temporary workman shall not be terminated as a punishment unless he has been given an opportunity of explaining the charges of misconduct alleged against him in the manner prescribed in Paragraph 14.

(3) Where the employment of any workmen is terminated, the wages earned by him and other dues, if any, shall be paid before the expiry of the second working day from the day on which his employment is terminated.

14. Disciplinary action for misconduct.--(1) A workman may be fined up to two per cent of his wages in a month for the following acts and omissions, namely:

_____

_____

Note.--Specify the acts and omissions which the employer may notify with the previous approval of the Government or of the prescribed authority in pursuance of section 8 of the Payment of Wages Act, 1936.

(2) A workman may be suspended for a period not exceeding four days at a time, or dismissed without notice or any compensation in lieu of notice, if he is found to be guilty of misconduct.

(3) The following acts and omissions shall be treated as misconduct.

(a) willful in subordination or disobedience, whether alone or in combination with others, to any lawful and reasonable order of a superior,

(b) theft, fraud or dishonesty in connection with the employer's business or property,

(c) willful damage to or loss of employer's goods or property,

(d) taking or giving bribes or any illegal gratification,

(e) habitual absence without leave or absence without leave for more than 10 days,

(f) habitual late attendance,

(g) habitual breach of any law applicable to the establishment,

(h) riotous or disorderly behaviors during working hours at the establishment or any act subversive of discipline,

(i) habitual negligence or neglect of work,

(j) frequent repetition of any act or omission for which a fine may be imposed to a maximum of 2 per cent of the wages in a month.

(k) striking work or inciting others to strike work in contravention of the provision of any law, or rule having the force of law.

(4) (a) Where a disciplinary proceeding against a workman is contemplated or is pending or where criminal proceedings against him in respect of any offence are under investigation or trial and the employer is satisfied that it is necessary or desirable to place the workman under suspension, he may, by order in writing suspend him with effect from such date as may be specified in the order. A statement setting out in detail the reasons for such suspension shall be supplied to the workman within a week from the date of suspension.

(b) A workman who is placed under suspension under Cl. (a) shall, during the period of such suspension, be paid a subsistence allowance at the following rates, namely:

(i) Where the enquiry contemplated or pending is departmental, the subsistence allowance shall, for the first ninety days from the date of suspension, be equal to one-half of the basic wages, dearness allowance and other compensatory allowances to which the workmen would have been entitled if he were on leave with wages. It the departmental enquiry gets prolonged and the workman continues to be under suspension for a period exceeding ninety days, the subsistence allowance shall for such period be equal to three-fourths of such basic wages dearness allowance and other compensatory allowances:

Provided that where such enquiry is prolonged beyond a period of ninety days for reasons directly attributable to the workman, the subsistence allowance shall, for the period exceeding ninety days, be reduced to one-fourth of such basic wages, dearness allowance and other compensatory allowances.

(ii) Where the enquiry is by an outside agency or, as the case may be, where criminal proceedings against workman are under investigation or trial, the subsistence allowance shall, for the first one hundred and eighty days from the date of suspension, be equal to one half of his basic wages, dearness allowance and other compensatory allowances to which the workman would have been entitled to if he was on leave. If such enquiry or criminal proceedings gets prolonged and the workman continues to be under suspension for a period exceeding one hundred and eighty days, the subsistence allowance shall for such period be equal to three-fourths of such wages:

Provided that where such enquiry or criminal proceeding is prolonged beyond a period of one hundred and eighty days for reasons directly attributable to the workman, the subsistence allowance shall, for the period exceeding one hundred and eighty days, be reduced to one-fourth of such wages.

(b-a) In the enquiry, the workman shall be entitled to appear in person or to be represented by an office-bearer of a trade union of which he is a member.

(b-b) The proceedings of the enquiry shall be recorded in Hindi or in English, the language of the State where the industrial establishment is located, whichever is preferred by the workman.

(b-c) The proceedings of the inquiry shall be completed within a period of three months :

Provided that the period of three months may, for reasons to be recorded in writing, be extended by such further period as may be deemed necessary by the inquiry officer.

(c) If on the conclusion of the enquiry or, as the case may be, of the criminal proceedings, the workman has been found guilty of the charges framed against him and it is considered, after giving the workman concerned a reasonable opportunity of making representation on the penalty proposed, that an order of dismissal or suspension or fine or stoppage of annual increment or reduction in rank would meet the ends of justice, the employer shall pass an order accordingly:

Provided that when an order of dismissal is passed under this clause, the workman shall be deemed to have been absent from duty during the period of suspension and shall not be entitled to any remuneration for such period, and the subsistence allowance already paid to him shall not be recovered :

Provided further that where the period between the date on which the workman was suspended from duty pending the inquiry or investigation or trial and the date on which an order or suspension was passed under this clause exceeds four days, the workman shall be deemed to have been suspended only for four days or for such shorter period as is specified in the said order of suspension and for the remaining period he shall be entitled to the same wages as he would have received if he had not been placed under suspension, after deducting the subsistence allowance paid to him for such period :

Provided also that where an order imposing fine or stoppage of annual increment or reduction in rank is passed under this clause, the workman shall be deemed to have been on duty during the period of suspension and shall be entitled to the same wages as he would have received if he had not been placed under suspension, after deducting the subsistence allowance paid to him for such period:

Provided also that in the case of a workman to whom the provisions of clause (2) of Article 311 of the Constitution apply, the provisions of that article shall be complied with.

(d) If on the conclusion of the inquiry, or as the case may be, or the criminal proceedings, the workman has been found to be not guilty of any of the charges framed against him, he shall be deemed to have been on duty during the period of suspension and shall be entitled to the same wages as he would have received if he had not been placed under suspension after deducting the subsistence allowance paid to him for such period.

(e) The payment of subsistence allowance under this standing order shall be subject to the workman concerned not taking up any employment during the period of suspension.

(5) In awarding punishment under this standing order, the authority imposing the punishment shall take into account any gravity of the misconduct, the previous record, if any, of the workman and any other extenuating or aggravating circumstances, that may exist. A copy of the order passed by the authority imposing the punishment shall be supplied to the workman concerned.

(6) (a) A workman aggrieved by an order imposing punishment may within twenty-one days from the date of receipt of the order, appeal to the appellate authority.

(b) The employer shall, for the purposes of Cl. (a) specify the appellate authority.

(c) The appellate authority, after giving an opportunity to the workman of being heard shall pass order as he thinks proper on the appeal within fifteen days of its receipt and communicate the same to the workman in writing.

15. Complaints.--All complaints arising out of employment including those relating to unfair treatment or wrongful exaction on the part of the employer or his agent, shall be submitted to the manager or other person specified in this behalf with the right of appeal to the employer.

16. Certificate on termination of service.--Every permanent workman shall be entitled to a service certificate at the time of his dismissal, discharge or retirement from service.

NOTE. - There is a provision under this Act for issuing a service certificate at the time of dismissal, discharge or retirement and every person is entitled to take such certificate.

17. Liability of employer--The employer of the establishment shall personally be held responsible for the proper and faithful observance of the standing orders.

17-A. (1) Any person desiring to prefer an appeal in pursuance of sub-section(1) of Section 6 of the Act shall draw up a memorandum of appeal setting out the ground of appeal and forward it in quintuplicate to the appellate authority accompanied by a Certified copy of the standing orders, amendments or modifications, as the case may be.

(2) The appellate authority shall, after giving the appellant an opportunity of being heard, confirm the standing orders, amendments or modifications as certified by the certifying officer unless it considers that there are reasons for giving the other parties to the proceedings a hearing before a final decision is made in the appeal.

(3) Where the appellate authority does not confirm the standing orders, amendments or modifications it shall fix a date for the hearing of the appeal and direct notice thereof to be given—

(a) where the appeal is filed by the employer or a workman, to trade unions of the workmen of the industrial establishments, and where there are no such trade unions to the representatives of workman elected under Cl. (b) of rule 6, or as the case may be, to the employer ;

(b) where the appeal is filed by a trade union to the employer and all other trade unions of the workmen of the industrial establishment ;

(c) where the appeal is filed by the representatives of the workmen, to the employer and any other workman whom the appellate authority joins as a party to the appeal.

(4) The appellant shall furnish each of the respondents with a copy of the memorandum of appeal.

(5) The appellate authority may at any stage call for any evidence it considers necessary for the disposal of the appeal.

(6) On the date fixed, under sub-rule (3) for the hearing of the appeal, the appellate authority shall take such evidence as it may have called for or consider to be relevant.

18. Exhibition of standing orders.--A copy of these orders in English and in Hindi shall be pasted on a notice-board maintained at or near the main entrance to the establishment and shall be kept in a legible condition.

[SCHEDULE I - A]
MODEL STANDING ORDERS FOR INDUSTRIAL ESTABLISHMENT IN COAL MINES

1. These orders shall come into force on............

2. Definition.--In these orders, unless the context otherwise requires-

(a) 'attendance' means presence of the workman concerned at the place or places where by the terms of his employment he is required to report for work and getting his attendance marked ;

(b) The expression 'employer' and 'workman' shall have the meanings assigned to them in Section 2(d) and

(c) 'Manager' means the manager of the mine and includes an acting manager for the time being appointed in accordance with rules

(d) words importing masculine gender shall be taken to include females; in the singular shall include the plural and *vice versa.*

3. Classification of workmen.--(a) "Workmen" shall be classified as -

(i) permanent;

(ii) Probationers;

(iii) *badlis* or substitute;

(iv) temporary;

(v) apprentices ;and

(vi) casual.

(b) A "permanent workman" is one who is appointed for an unlimited period or who has satisfactorily put in three months' continuous service in a permanent post as a probationer;

(c) A "probationer" is one who is provisionally employed to fill a vacancy in a permanent post and has not completed three months' service in that post unless the probationary period is extended. If a permanent workmen is employed as a probationer in a new post he may, at any time, during the probationary period not exceeding three months, be reverted to his old permanent post unless the probationary period is extended.

(d) A '*badli*' or substitute is one who is appointed in the post of a permanent workman or a probationer who is temporarily absent :but he would cease to be a 'Badli" on completion of a continuous period of service of one year 190 attendances in the case of below ground workman and 240 attendances in the case of any other workman) in the same post or other post or posts in the same category or earlier

168

if the post is vacated by the permanent workman or probationer. A *"badli"* working in place of a probationer would be deemed to be permanent after completion of the probationary period.

(e) A "temporary" workman is a workman who has been engaged for work which is of an essentially temporary nature likely to be finished within a limited period. The period within which it is likely to be finished should also be specified but it may be extended from time to time, if necessary.

(f) An "apprentice" is a learner who is either paid an allowance or not paid any allowance during the period of his training, which shall *inter alia* be specified in his term of contract.

(g) A "casual" workman is a workman who has been engaged for work which is of an essentially casual nature.

4. Every workman shall be given a ticket appropriate to his classification at the time of his appointment and shall, on being required to do so, show it to the person authorized by the employer in that behalf. The said ticket shall carry the signature or thumb-impression of the workman concerned. If the workman looses his ticket, the Manager shall provide him with another ticket on a payment of 25 paisa.

5. Display of notices.--(a) The period and hours of work for all classes of workmen in each shift shall be exhibited in English and the language understood by the majority of workmen employed in the establishment on notice-boards maintained at or near the main entrance of the establishment and at the time-keeper's office, if any (b) Notices, specifying (a) the days observed by the establishment as holidays and (b) pay days shall be posted on the said Notice-boards, (c) notices specifying the rates of wages and scales of allowances payable to all classes of workmen and for all classes of work shall be displayed on the said notice-boards.

6. Payment of wages.--(a) Wages shall be paid direct to the individual workmen on any working day between the hours 6.00 a.m. and 6.00 p.m. at the office of the mine. The manager or any other responsible person authorized by him shall witness and attest the payments and note the date of payment in the wage register. Payment of wages to a contractor's workman shall be made at a place to be specified by the manager and it shall be witnessed by a nominee of the employer deputed for this purpose in writing.

(b) Any wages due to a workman but not paid on the usual pay day on account of their being unclaimed shall be paid by the employer on such unclaimed wage pay day in each week as may be notified to the workmen. If the workman so desires, the unpaid wages and other dues payable to him shall be remitted to his address by money order after deducting there from the money order commission charges. All claims for the unpaid wages shall be presented to the employer within a period of twelve months from the date on which the wages become due.

(c) Overtime shall be worked and wages thereof paid in accordance with the provisions of the Mines Act, 1952, as amended by the Mines (Amendment) Act, 1959, and as may be prescribed from time to time. For work on weekly rest day, the workman shall be paid as laid down in any agreement or award or as the case may be, as per usage or custom.

7. Shift working.--More than one shift may be worked in a department or departments of any section of a department of the establishment at the discretion of the employer. If more than one shift is worked a workman shall be liable to be transferred from one shift to another. No shift working shall be discontinued without two months' notice being given in writing to the workmen prior to such discontinuance; provided that no such notice shall be necessary if the closing of the shift is under an agreement with the workman affected. If as a result of the discontinuance of shift working, any workmen are to be retrenched, such retrenchment shall be effected in accordance with the provisions of the Industrial Disputes Act, 1947 (14 of 1947), and the rules made there under. If shift working is restarted, the workmen shall be given notice and re-employed in accordance with the provisions of the said Act and the said rules.

8. Attendance.--All workmen shall be at work at the mine at the time fixed and notified to them.

9. Absence from place of work.--Any workman, who after going underground or after coming to his work in the department in which he is employed, is found absent from his proper place of work during working hours without permission from the appropriate authority or without any sufficient reason shall be liable to be treated as absent for the period of his absence.

10. Festival holidays and leave.--(a) There shall be seven paid festival holidays or as laid down in an agreement or an award in force. Out of these seven days, the Republic Day, Independence Day and Mahatma Gandhi's Birthday shall be allowed without option and the rest of the days shall be fixed by agreement or local custom. Whenever a workman has to work on any of these holidays, he shall, at his option be entitled to either thrice the wages for the day or twice the wages for the day on which he work and in addition to avail himself of a substituted holiday with wages on any other day or as laid down in an agreement or an award in force.

(b) (i)The workmen shall be entitled to leave with wages in accordance with the provisions contained in Chapter VII of Mines Act, 1952.

(ii) Normally a workman will not be refused the leave applied for by him. But the employer may refuse, revoke or curtail the leave applied for by workman, if the exigencies of work so demand. Wages in lieu of leave shall be paid to a workman, where he has been refused the leave asked for and in cases where he cannot accumulate the leave any further. If a workman is refused leave in a particular year in the interest of work, it would be open to him next year either to avail of leave on two occasions with the usual railway concession or in case he avails of leave only on one occasion the railway fare for the unveiled trip would be paid to him in the shape of National Savings/National Defence Certificates.

(c) Quarantine leave shall be granted to a workman, who is prevented from attending to his duty because of his coming into contact, through no fault of his own, with a person suffering from a contagious disease. The leave shall be granted for such period as is covered by a certificate from the medical officer of the mine. Payment for the period of quarantine leave shall be at the rate of 50 percent of the wages (basic plus dearness allowance) payable to a workman. Quarantine leave cannot be claimed, if a workman has refused to accept during the previous three months prophylactic treatment for the disease in question.

(d) A workman who desires to obtain leave of absence shall apply to the manager not less than fifteen days before the commencement of the leave, except where leave is required in unforeseen circumstances, and the manager shall issue orders on the application within a week of its submission of two days prior to the commencement of the leave applied for, whichever is earlier: provided that if the leave applied for is to commence on the date of the application within three days thereof, orders shall be given on the same day. If the leave asked for is granted, a leave pass shall be given to the workman. If the leave is refused or postponed, the fact of such refusal or postponement and the reasons therefore shall be recorded in writing in a register to be maintained for the purpose, and if the worker so desires a copy of the entry in the register shall be supplied to him. If the workman after proceeding on leave desires an extension thereof, he shall apply to the manager, who shall send a written reply either granting or refusing extension of leave to the workman. Sanction/refusal of leave should be communicated to the workman in writing invariably.

(e) If a workman remains absent beyond the period of leave originally granted or subsequently extended, he shall lose lien on his appointment unless he-

(i) returns within ten days of expiry of his leave; and

(ii) explains to the satisfaction of the manager his inability to return on the expiry of his leave. In case, the workman loses, as aforesaid, his lien on his appointment, he shall be entitled to be kept on the "*badly* list".

(f) A workman may be granted casual leave of absence with pay not exceeding five days in the aggregate in a calendar year. Such leave shall not be for more than three days at a time except in case of sickness. Such leave is intended to meet special circumstances which cannot be foreseen. Ordinarily the previous permission of the head of the department in the establishment, shall be obtained before such leave is taken, but where this is not possible, the head of the department shall, as soon as may be practicable, be informed in writing of such absence and of the probable duration thereof.

(g) Notwithstanding anything mentioned above, any workman who overstays his sanctioned leave or remains absent without reasonable cause will render himself liable for disciplinary action.

11. Medical aid in case of accident.- Where a workman meets with an accident in the course of and arising out of his employment, the employer shall make satisfactory arrangements for immediate and necessary medical aid to the injured workman free of cost and shall arrange for prompt payment of compensation admissible under the Workmen's Compensation Act, covering also the first three days of absence on account of injury.

12. Railway travel facilities.--(a) When a workman proceeds on leave and is qualified for free railway fare, the employer shall give him the cost equivalent of his ticket (including bus fare) and for boat to his home.

(b) Every workman who has completed a period of twelve months' continuous service, would qualify for railway fare or bus fare or both for going home on leave and returning to the mine on the expiry of the leave. The twelve months' service shall be deemed to have been completed if, during the twelve months preceding the date on which he applies for leave, he has worked for not less than two hundred and forty days.

(c) If on the expiry of the leave, a workman returns he shall then receive a cash payment equivalent to the return fare. If on his return the mine is unable to have him back, he shall be paid return fare at once.

(d) If the journey home is by bus or partly by bus and partly by train, the cost of journey shall be adjusted accordingly.

(e) The workman shall be entitled to railway fare by mail or express train, wherever under the Railway Rules tickets are available for such travel.

(f) The class by witch a workman is entitled to travel shall be:

(i) if his basic wage is Rs. 165 or less per month III Class.

(ii) if his basic wage is above Rs.165 and up to Rs. 265 per month II Class.

(iii) if his basic wage is above Rs. 265 per moth I Class.

13. Termination of services.--(a)For terminating the services of permanent workman having less than one year of continuous service, notice of one month in writing with reasons or wages in lieu thereof shall be given by the employer:

Provided that no such notice shall be required to be given when the services of the workman are terminated on account of misconduct established in accordance with the Standing Orders.

(b) Subject to the provisions of the Industrial Disputes Act, 1947 no notice of termination of employment shall be necessary in the case of temporary and Badli workmen:

Provided that a temporary workman, who has completed three months continuous service, shall be given two weeks' notice of the intention to terminate his employment if such termination is not in accordance with the terms of the contract of his employment :

Provided further that when the services of a temporary workman, who has not completed three months' continuous service, are terminated before the completion of the term of employment given to him, he shall be informed of the reasons in writing. When the services of a badli workman are terminated before the return to work of the permanent incumbent or the expiry of his badli's term of employment, he shall be informed of the reasons for such termination in writing.

(c) No workman shall leave the service of an employer unless notice in writing is given at the scale indicated below-

(i) For monthly paid workmen One month.

(ii) For weekly paid workmen Two weeks:

Provided that it will be for employer to relax this condition and the workman may pay cash in lieu of such notice.

(d) For purposes of Standing Orders 13 (a), (b) and (c) the terms 'service' and 'wages' shall have the same meaning as assigned to them in Sec. 25 (B) (1) and 2 (rr) respectively of the Industrial Disputes Act, 1947.

14. Stoppage of work and re-opening.--(a) Subject to the provisions of Chapter V-A of the Industrial Disputes Act, 1947, the employer may, at any time, in the event of underground trouble, fire, catastrophe, breakdown of machinery, stoppage of power supply, epidemic, civil commotion or any other cause beyond the control of the employer, stop any section or sections of the mine wholly or partly for any period or periods.

(b) In the event of such stoppage during working hours, the workmen affected shall be notified by notice put up on the notice-board in the departments concerned and of the office as soon as practicable as to when work will be resumed and whether they are to remain or leave their place of work. The workmen will not ordinarily be required to remain for more than two hours after the commencement of the stoppage. Whenever workmen are laid off on account of failure of plant or a temporary curtailment of production or other causes they shall be paid compensation in accordance with the provisions of the Industrial Disputes, Act, 1947. Where no such compensation is admissible, they shall be granted leave with or without wages as the case may be, at the option of the workman concerned, leave with wages being granted to the extent of any leave due to them. When workmen are to be laid off for an indefinitely long period, their services may be terminated subject to the provisions of the Industrial Disputes Act, 1947.If normal work is resumed two weeks' notice thereof shall be given by the pasting of notices at or near the mine office and the workmen discharged either by the employer shall if they present themselves for work, have preference for employment.

(c) The employer may in the event of a strike affecting either wholly or partially any section of the mine close down either wholly or partially such section of the mine and any other section affected by such closure. The fact of such closure shall be notified by notices put up on notice-board in the manager's office. Prior to resumption of work, the workmen concerned will be notified by a general notice indicating as to when work will be resumed. A copy of such notice shall be sent to the registered trade union or unions functioning in the establishment.

15. Method of filling vacancies.--In the matter of filling up of permanent vacancies, *badli* and temporary workmen and probationers would be given preference in order of their seniority.

16. Transfers.- Workmen may be transferred due to exigencies of work from one department to another or from one station to another or from one coal mine to another under the same ownership provided that the pay, grade, continuity and other conditions of service of the workman are not adversely affected by such transfer and provided also that if a workman is transferred from one job to another, that job should be of similar nature and such as he is capable of doing and provided further that (i) reasonable notice is given of such transfers and (ii) reasonable joining time is allowed in case of transfers from one station to another. The workman concerned shall be paid the actual transport charges plus 50 per cent, thereof to meet incidental charges.

17. Disciplinary action for misconduct.--(i) A workman may be suspended or fined or his increment may be stopped or he may be demoted or dismissed without notice if he is found to be guilty of misconduct under this standing order, provided that suspension without pay as a punishment shall not exceed ten days. The workman may be suspended pending departmental enquiry and in such cases he shall be paid a subsistence allowance equal to half his wages as defined in the Payment of Wages Act 1936, for the period of suspension up to 30 days. If, however, he is kept suspended by the management beyond 30 days his subsistence allowance will be at the rate of 3/4th of his wages as aforesaid but if the enquiry is delayed beyond the 30 days because of the workman, the subsistence allowance shall be reduced to 1/4th of his wages. The employer shall normally complete the enquiry within ten days. The payment of subsistence allowance will be subject to his not taking any employment elsewhere during the suspension period.

The following shall denote misconduct:

(a) Theft, fraud, or dishonesty in connection with the employer's business or property.

(b) Taking or giving of bribes or an illegal gratification whatsoever in connection with the employer's business or his own interests.

(c) Willful insubordination or disobedience, whether alone or in conjunction with another or others, or of any lawful or reasonable order of a superior. The order of the superior should normally be in writing.

(d) Habitual late attendance and habitual absence without leave or without sufficient cause.

(e) Drunkenness, fighting or riotous, disorderly or indecent behaviors while on duty at the place of work.

(f) Habitual neglect of work.

(g) Habitual indiscipline.

(h) Smoking underground within the area in places where it is prohibited.

(i) Causing willful damage to work in progress or to property of the employer.

(j) Sleeping on duty.

(k) Malingering or showing down work.

(l) Acceptance of gifts from subordinate employees.

(m) Conviction in any Court of Law for any criminal offence involving moral turpitude.

(n) Continuous absence without permission and without satisfactory cause for more than ten days.

(o) Giving false information regarding one's name, age, father's name, qualification or previous service at the time of the employment.

(p) Leaving work without permission or sufficient reason.

(q) Any breach of the Mines Act, 1952, or any other Act or any rules, regulations or bye-laws there under, or of any Standing Orders.

(r) Threatening, abusing or assaulting any superior or co-worker.

(s) Habitual money-lending.

(t) Preaching of or inciting to violence.

(u) Abetment of or attempt at abetment of any of the above acts of misconduct.

(v) Going on illegal strike either singly or with other workers with out giving 14 day's previous notice.

(w) Disclosing to any unauthorized person of any confidential information in regard to the working or process of the establishment which may come into the possession of the workman in the course of his work.

(x) Refusal to accepted any charge-sheet or order or notice communicated in writing.

(y) Failure or refusal to wear or use any protective equipment given by the employers.

(ii) No order of punishment under Standing Order No. 17 (i) shall be made unless the workman concerned is informed in writing of the alleged misconduct and is given an opportunity to explain the allegations made against him.

A departmental enquiry shall be instituted before dealing with the charges. During the period of enquiry, the workman concerned may be suspended. The workman may take the assistance of a co-worker to help him in the enquiry, if he so desires. The records of the departmental enquiry shall be kept in writing. The approval of the owner, agent or the Chief Mining Engineer of the employer or a person holding similar position shall be obtained before imposing the punishment of dismissal. At the end of the enquiry proceedings shall be given to the workman concerned on the conclusion of the enquiry, on request by the workman.

(iii) If a workman is not found guilty of the charges framed against him, he shall be deemed to be on duty during the full period of his suspension and he shall be entitled to receive the same wages as he would have received if he had not been suspended.

(iv) In awarding punishment under this Standing Order, the authority awarding punishment shall take into account the gravity of the misconduct, the previous record, if any, of the workman and any other extenuating or aggravating circumstances that may exist. A copy of the order passed by the authority awarding punishment shall be supplied to the workman concerned.

18. Time-limit for making complaints, appeals, etc.- All complaints arising out of employment including those relating to unfair treatment or wrongful exaction on the part of the employer or his servant shall be submitted within 7 days of such cause of complaint to the manager of the mine, with the right of appeal to the employer. Any appeal to the employer shall be made within 3 days of the decision of the manager. The employer shall normally give his decision within three days of the receipt of the appeal.

19. Liability of manager of the mine. - The manager of the mine shall personally be held responsible for the proper enforcement of these standing orders provided that where a manager is overruled by his superior the latter shall be held responsible for the decision taken.

20. Service certificate.- Every workman who was employed continuously for a period of more than three months shall be entitled to a service certificate at the time of his leaving the service of employer.

21. Entry and exit.- All workmen shall enter and leave the premises of the establishment through authorized gates and shall be liable for search while going in or coming out of the premises. In case of women workmen search will only be made by women.

22. Exhibition and supply of Standing Orders.- A copy of these orders in English and in the regional languages of the local area in which the mine is situated shall be posted at the manager's office and in such other places of the mine as the employer may decide and it shall be kept in a legible condition. A copy of the standing orders shall be supplied to a workman on application, on payment of a reasonable price. A trade union in the establishment will, however, be entitled to the free supply of a copy of the standing orders, provided the union is one which is recognized by the employer.

23 SCHEDULE I-B

Model Standing Orders on additional items applicable to all industries

(1) SERVICE RECORD

Matters relating to service card, token tickets, certification of service, change of residential address of workers and record of age.

(i) *Service Card.*- Every industrial establishment shall maintain a service card in respect of each workman in the form appended to these orders, wherein particulars of that workman shall be recorded with the knowledge of that workman and duly attested by an officer authorized in this behalf together with date.

(ii) *Certification of service.*- Every workman shall be entitled to a service certificate, specifying the nature of work (designation) and the period of employment (indicating the days, months, years), at the time of discharge, termination, retirement or resignation from service;

(iii) *Residential address of workman.-* A workman shall notify the employer immediately on engagement the details of his residential address and thereafter promptly communicate to his employer any change of his residential address. In case the workman has not communicated to his employer the change in his residential address, his last known address shall be treated by the employer as his residential address for sending any communication.

(iv) *Record of age.-* (a) Every workman shall indicate his exact date of birth to the employer or the officer authorised by him in this behalf, at the time of entering service of the establishment. The employer or the officer authorised by him in this behalf may before the date of birth of a workman is entered in his, service card, require him to supply :-

(i) his matriculation or school leaving certificate granted by the Board of Secondary Education or similar educational authority; or

(ii) a certified copy of his date of birth as recorded in the registers of a municipality, local authority or Panchayat or Registrar of Births;

(iii) in the absence of either of the aforesaid two categories of certificate, the employer or the officer authorized by him in this behalf may require the workman to supply, a certificate from a Government Medical Officer not below the rank of an Assistant Surgeon indicating the probable age of the workman provided the cost of obtaining such certificate is borne by the employer;

(iv) where it is not practicable to obtain a certificate from a Government Medical Officer, an affidavit sworn, either by the workman or his parents, or by a near relative, who is in a position to know about the workman's actual or approximate date of birth, before a first Class Magistrate or Oath Commissioner, as evidence in support of the date of birth given by him.

(b) The date of birth of a workman, once entered in the service card of the establishment shall be the sole evidence of his age in relation to all matters pertaining to his service including fixation of the date of his retirement from the service of the establishment. All formalities regarding recording of the date of birth shall be finalised within three months of the appointment of a workman.

(c) Cases where date of birth of any workman had already been decided on the date these rules come into force shall not be reopened under these provisions.

Note. - Where exact date of birth is not available and the year of birth is only established then the 1st July of the said year shall be taken as the date of birth.

(2) CONFIRMATION

The employer shall in accordance with the terms and conditions stipulated in the letter of appointment, confirm the eligible workman and issue a letter of confirmation to him. Whenever a workman is confirmed, an entry with regard to the confirmation shall also be made in his service card within a period of thirty days from the date of such confirmation.

(3) AGE OF RETIREMENT

The age of retirement or superannuation of a workman shall be as may be agreed upon between the employer and the workman under an agreement or as specified in a settlement or award which is binding on both the workman and the employer. Where there is no such agreed age, retirement or superannuation shall be on completion of [58] years of age by the workman.

(4) TRANSFER

A workman may be transferred according to exigencies of work from one shop or department to another or from one station to another or from one establishment to another under the same employer:

Provided that the wages, grade, continuity of service and other conditions of service of the workman are not adversely affected by such transfer:.

Provided further that a workman is transferred from one job to another, which he is capable of doing, and provided also that where the transfer involves moving from one State to another such transfer shall take place, either with the consent of the workman or where there is a specific provision to that effect in the letter of appointment, and provided also that (i) reasonable notice is given to such workman, and (ii) reasonable joining time is allowed in case of transfers from one station to another. The workman concerned shall be paid traveling allowance including the transport charges, and fifty per cent thereof to meet incidental charges.

(5) MEDICAL AID IN CASE OF ACCIDENTS

Where a workman meets with an accident in the course of or arising out of his employment, the employer shall, at the employer's expense, make satisfactory arrangements for immediate and necessary medical aid to the injured workman and shall arrange for his further treatment, if considered necessary by the doctor attending on him.

Wherever the workman is entitled for treatment and benefits under the Employee's State Insurance Act, 1948 or the Workman's Compensation Act, 1923, the employer shall arrange for the treatment and compensation accordingly.

(6) MEDICAL EXAMINATION

Wherever the recruitment rules specify medical examination of a workman on, his first appointment, the employer, shall, at the employer's expense make arrangements for the medical examination by a registered medical practitioner.

(7) SECRECY

No workman shall take any papers, books, drawings, photographs, instruments, apparatus, documents or any other property of an industrial establishment out of the work premises except with the written permission of his immediate superior, nor shall he in any way pass or cause to be passed or disclose or cause to be disclosed any information or matter concerning the manufacturing process, trade secrets and confidential documents of the establishment to any unauthorized person, company or corporation without the written permission of the employer.

(8) EXCLUSIVE SERVICE

A workman shall not at any time work against the interest of the industrial establishment in which he is employed and shall not take any employment in addition to his job in the establishment, which may adversely affect the interest of his employer.

INDUSTRIAL DISPUTES ACT, 1947:

Some of the provisions of the Industrial Disputes Act, 1947 are directly related to domestic enquiry. As a matter of fact, discharge, dismissal, and retrenchment as well as the authorities having dispute resolution powers like Conciliation officers, Arbitrators, Industrial Tribunal, Labour Court, Tribunal and National Tribunal are mentioned in the Industrial Disputes Act. It is imperative to look into the provisions of the Industrial Disputes Act having a bearing on domestic enquiry.

DISMISSAL OF AN INDIVIDUAL WORKMAN TO BE DEEMED TO BE AN INDUSTRIAL DISPUTE :

Section 2A of the Industrial Disputes Act mentions that the dismissal of an individual workman will come within the ambit of industrial dispute. Where any employer discharges, dismisses, retrenches or otherwise terminates the services of an individual workman, any such dispute or difference between that workman and his employer connected with, or arising out of, such discharge, dismissal, retrenchment or termination shall be deemed to be an industrial dispute notwithstanding that no other workman nor any union of workmen is a party to the dispute.

It restricts the power of the employers to victimize any particular workman. It is also not required that the cause of such discharged or dismissed workman should be upheld by workmen collectively, or by any trade union. The lone employee who has been wrongly discharged or dismissed can fight against capricious or arbitrary action of the employer. The law courts will take up the cause of individual workman considering it to be an industrial dispute.

Any wrong termination of service of a workman by the employer has the potential to disturb the industrial relations scenario. The principal act of the Labour Court and the Tribunal is to give impetus to peaceful industrial relations as well as to mitigate the suffering of a workman by the hands of an atrocious employer. Section 2A of the Industrial Disputes Act fulfills this purpose.

MATTERS WITHIN THE JURISDICTION OF INDUSTRIAL TRIBUNAL AND LABOUR COURT

The jurisdiction of the Labour Court and Industrial Tribunal has been mentioned in Section 7 and Section 7 A respectively of the Industrial Disputes Act. As a matter of fact, a case of discharge or dismissal can be referred by the government to either of the two authorities. However, the industrial tribunal has more powers as it can mitigate the punishment awarded to a delinquent employee by his employer. The second schedule of the Industrial Disputes Act deals with the jurisdictional powers of the Labour Court. The third schedule of the Industrial Disputes Act deals with the jurisdictional powers of the Industrial Tribunal.

MATTERS WITHIN THE JURISDICTION OF LABOUR COURTS

The propriety or legality of an order passed by an employer under the standing orders;
- The application and interpretation of standing orders;
- Discharge or dismissal of workmen including reinstatement of, or grant of relief to, workmen wrongfully dismissed;
- Withdrawal of any customary concession or privilege;
- Illegality or otherwise of a strike or lock out; and
- All matters other than those specified in the third schedule.

MATTERS WITHIN THE JURISDICTION OF INDUSTRIAL TRIBUNAL

- Wages, including the period and mode of payment;
- Compensatory and other allowances;
- Hours of work and rest intervals;
- Leave with wages and holidays;
- Bonus, profit sharing, provident fund and gratuity;
- Shift working otherwise than in accordance with standing orders;
- Classification by grades;
- Rules of discipline;
- Rationalization;
- Retrenchment of workmen and closure of establishment, and;
- Any other matter that may be prescribed.

POWERS OF LABOUR COURT AND TRIBUNALS TO GIVE APPROPRIATE RELIEF TO A DISCHARGED OR DISMISSED WORKMAN:

Where an industrial dispute relating to the discharge or dismissal of a workman is referred to a Labour Court or Tribunal for adjudication, and the Labour Court or Tribunal is satisfied that the order of discharge or dismissal was not justified it may by it's award set aside the order of discharge or dismissal and direct reinstatement of the workman on such terms and conditions, if any, as it thinks fit, or give such other relief to the workman including the awards of any lesser punishment in lieu of discharge or dismissal as the circumstances of the case may require.

Provided that in any such proceeding the Labour Court or the Tribunal shall rely only on the materials on record and shall not take any fresh evidence in relation to the matter.

PAYMENT OF FULL WAGES TO DISCHARGED OR DISMISSED WORKMAN WHEN PROCEEDING IS PENDING IN HIGHER COURT:

It is mentioned in Section 17 B of the Industrial Disputes Act that where in any case Labour Court or Tribunal by its award directs reinstatement of any workman and the employer prefers any proceedings against such award in a High Court or the Supreme Court, the employer shall be liable to pay such workman, during the period of pendency of such proceedings in the High Court or the Supreme Court, full wages last drawn by him, inclusive of any maintenance allowance admissible to him under any rule if the workman had not been employed in any establishment during such period and an affidavit by such workman had been filed to that effect in such court.

Provided that where it is proved to the satisfaction of the High Court or Supreme Court that such workman had been employed and had been receiving adequate remuneration during any such period or part thereof, the Court shall order that no wages shall be payable for such period or part thereof, as the case may be.

The provision of Section 17 B provides adequate relief to a discharged or dismissed workman because the lengthy legal battle an employer can bear, but it may not be possible for the workman to withstand the difficulties in absence of any financial support. Moreover, this could also be a trick in the hands of an unkind employer to harass a workman by pulling him into a long drawn legal battle in High Court or Supreme Court pending his reinstatement. But, the provision of section 17 B thwarts that motive.

UNFAIR LABOUR PRACTICE AND VICTIMIZATION AS CAUSE OF DISCHARGE AND DISMISSAL OF WORKMAN:

Dismissal and discharge or workmen is often related to victimization and unfair labour practice by the employer, or a retaliation of the employer of the unfair labour practice on the part of workman. The term 'victimization' has not been dealt in Industrial Disputes Act or any other statute except a casual mention of the word in unfair labour practice by the employer as mentioned in Schedule V of the Industrial Disputes Act. The term unfair labour practice has, however, been mentioned in detail in Chapter V - C and Schedule V of the Industrial Disputes Act.

UNFAIR LABOUR PRACTICE :

Unfair labour practice has been prohibited and is subject to penalty under the Industrial Disputes Act. It is important to note what constitutes Unfair labour practice both on the part of the employer and that of the workmen as mentioned in Schedule V of the Industrial Disputes Act, 1947.

I. Unfair labour practices on the part of employers and trade unions of employers :

1. To interfere with, restraint from, or coerce, workmen in the exercise of their right to organize, form, join or assist a trade union or to engage in concerned activities for the purposes of collective bargaining or other mutual aid or protection, that is to say,-
   (a) threatening workmen with discharge or dismissal, if they join a trade union
   (b) threatening a lock out or closure if a trade union is organized; and
   (c) granting wage increase to workmen at crucial periods of trade union organization, with a view to undermining the efforts of the trade union at organization.
2. To dominate, interfere with or contribute support, financial or otherwise, to any trade union, that is to say,-
   (a) an employer taking an active interest in organizing a trade union of his workmen; and
   (b) an employer showing partiality or granting favour to one of several trade unions attempting to organize his workmen or to its members, where such a trade union is not a recognized trade union.
3. To establish employer-sponsored trade unions of workmen
4. To encourage or discourage membership in any trade union by discriminating against any workman, that is to say:-

(a) discharging or punishing a workman, because he urged other workmen to join or organize a trade union;

(b) discharging or dismissing a workman for taking part in any strike (not being a strike which is deemed to be an illegal strike under this Act);

(c) changing seniority rating of workmen because of trade union activities;

(d) refusing to promote workmen to higher posts on account of their trade union activities;

(e) giving unmerited promotions to certain workmen with a view to creating discord amongst other workmen, or to undermine the strength of their trade union;

(f) discharge office bearers or active members of the trade union on account of their trade union activities.

5. To discharge or dismiss workmen –

(a) by way of victimization;

(b) not in good faith, but in the colourable exercise of the employer's right;

(c) by falsely implicating a workman in a criminal case on false evidence or on concocted evidence;

(d) for patently false reasons;

(e) on untrue or trumpet up allegations of absence without leave;

(f) in utter disregard of the principles of natural justice in the conduct of domestic enquiry or with undue haste;

(g) for misconduct of a minor or technical character, without having any regard to the nature of the particular misconduct or the past record of service of the workman, thereby leading to a disproportionate punishment.

6. To abolish the work of a regular nature being done by workmen, and to give such work to contractors as a measure of breaking a strike.

7. To transfer a workman mala fide from one place to another, under the guise of following management policy.

8. To insist upon individual workmen, who are on a legal strike to sign a good conduct bond, as a pre-condition to allowing them to resume work.

9. To show favoritism or partiality to one set of workers regardless of merit.

10. To employ workmen as 'badlis', casuals or temporaries and to continue them as such for years, with the object of depriving them of the status and privileges of permanent workmen.

11. To discharge or discriminate against any workman for filing charges or testifying against an employer in any enquiry proceeding relating to any industrial dispute.
12. To recruit workmen during a strike which is not an illegal strike.
13. Failure to implement award, settlement or agreement.
14. To indulge in acts of force or violence.
15. To refuse to bargain collectively, in good faith with the recognized trade unions.
16. Proposing or continuing a lock- out deemed to be illegal under this Act.

II. Unfair labour practice on the part of workmen and trade unions of workmen

1. To advise or actively support or instigate any strike deemed to be illegal under the Act.
2. To coerce workmen in the exercise of their right to self-organization or to join a trade union or refrain from joining any trade union, that is to say-
   (a) for a trade union or its members to picketing in such a manner that non-striking workmen are physically debarred from entering the work places;
   (b) to indulge in acts of force or violence or to hold out threats of intimidation in connection with a strike against non-striking workmen or against managerial staff.
3. For a recognized union to refuse to bargain collectively in good faith with the employer.
4. To indulge in coercive activities against certification of bargaining representative.
5. To stage, encourage or instigate such forms of coercive actions as willful "go slow", squatting on the work premises after working hours or "*gherao*" of any of the members of the managerial or other staff.
6. To stage demonstrations at the residences of the employers or the managerial staff members.
7. To incite or indulge in willful damage to employer's property connected with the industry.
8. To indulge in acts of force or violence or to hold out threats of intimidation against any workman with a view to prevent him from attending work.

VICTIMIZATION

As mentioned earlier, Victimization has not been dealt with in any statute. The term finds a casual reference in unfair labour practice where it mentioned that a workman is discharge or dismissed by way of victimization as unfair labour practice by the employer. But, what is victimization and what are the possible reasons of victimization has not been mentioned anywhere. The study of the trend of punishment in Industries over the past years gives a comprehension of the term victimization.

As a matter of fact when an employee is punished and put to suffering without any fault on his part then in common parlance it is called victimization of that employee by his employer. The employee is victimized by the employer for hidden or unhidden reasons.

Victimization is generally related to trade union activities of the employee. But, in fact, there can be multiple reasons why an employee is victimized by the employer. Some of the reasons are mentioned below-

- Trade Union Activities of the employee
- Complaint about the employer to any government authority by the employee
- Opposition of any arbitrary action of the employer
- Refusal to support unlawful activities of the employer
- Refusal to accept unreasonable demands of the employer
- Opposition to Unfair labour practices of the employer
- Typical Indian cast and social group factors

Very often the real reasons of victimization do not surface, and are not reported by the workman. Majority of the victimization cases relate to trade union activities of the workman. Employees are also victimized when they oppose arbitrary and unlawful actions of the employer or the management.

When an employer victimizes an employee he tries to weed him out by taking disciplinary action against him on concocted of flimsy grounds. In such cases, the act of discharge, dismissal, or termination of service, which is ostensibly taken on other grounds, suffers from defect and shows colourable exercise of power by the employer.

It may be mentioned, however, that when an employee takes resort to unfair labour practice the employer has all the good reasons to dismiss him from the service.

REQUIREMENT TO TAKE PERMISSION FROM AUTHORITIES BEFORE DISCHARGE OR DISMISSAL DURING PENDENCY OF DISPUTE

The Industrial disputes Act in chapter VII (Miscellaneous) contains that conditions of service etc. of a workman has to remain unchanged under certain circumstances during the pendency of any dispute.

Conditions of service, etc. to remain unchanged under certain circumstances during pendency of proceedings.

Section 33 (I) states that during the pendency of any conciliation proceeding before a conciliation officer or a Board or of any proceeding before an arbitrator or a Labour Court or Tribunal or National Tribunal in respect of an industrial dispute, no employer shall –

(a) in regard to any matter connected with the dispute, alter to the prejudice of the workmen concerned in such dispute, the conditions of service applicable to them immediately before the commencement of such proceeding; or

(b) for any misconduct connected with the dispute, discharge or punish whether by dismissal or otherwise, any workmen concerned in such dispute, save with the express permission in writing of the authority before which the proceeding is pending.

(2) During the pendency of any such proceeding in respect of an industrial dispute, the employer may, in accordance with the standing orders applicable to a workman concerned in such dispute or, where there are no such standing orders, in accordance with the terms of the contract, whether express or implied, between him and the workman-

(a) alter in regard to any matter not connected with the dispute, the conditions of service applicable to that workman immediately before the commencement of such proceeding, or

(b) for any misconduct not connected with the dispute, discharge or punish, whether by dismissal or otherwise, that workman; Provided that no such workman shall be discharged or dismissed, unless he has been paid wages for one month and an application has been made by the employer to the authority before which the proceeding is pending for approval of action taken by the employer-

(3) Notwithstanding anything contained in section sub-section (2) no employer shall, during the pendency of any such proceeding in respect of an industrial dispute, take any action against any protected workman concerned in such dispute-

(a) by altering to the prejudice of such protected workman, the conditions of service applicable to him immediately before the commencement of such proceedings; or

(b) by discharging or punishing, whether by dismissal or otherwise, such protected workman,save with the express permission in writing of the authority before which the proceeding is pending.

Explanation: For the purposes of this sub-section, a "protected workman", in relation to an establishment, means a workman who, being a member of the executive or other office-bearer of a registered trade union connected with the establishment, is recognized as such in accordance with the rules made in this behalf.

■ It is clear, therefore, that during the pendency of a dispute the powers of the employer to punish a workman by discharge or dismissal or to bring any change in the conditions of service of workman who are affected by the dispute is fettered and the employer is required to take permission from the authorities before taking any disciplinary action.

■ It is also clear that action can be initiated against a protected workman also in case of pendency of dispute. However, the employer is required to take prior permission from the concerned authorities. An office bearer of a trade union, or a protected workman is also required to maintain discipline in the organization like any other workman, and by virtue of being a protected workman he does not fall outside the scope of a punitive action.

THE PUBLIC SERVANTS (INQUIRIES) ACT, 1850

The provisions of the Public Services (inquiries) Act, 1850 is very much in the Statute book along with the constitutional provisions relating to the government employees working in the civil capacity under the government. The provisions of the constitution has already been discussed at relevant places in this book. The provisions as mentioned in the Public Services Inquiries Act, however, needs to be mentioned in detail here.

The Public Servants (Inquiries) Act, 1850

(INDIA ACT XXXVII, 1850.) (1st November, 1850.)

For regulating inquiries into the behaviour of Public Servants.

Whereas it is expedient to amend the law for regulating inquires into the behaviour of public servants not removable from their appointments without the sanction of Government, and to make the same uniform throughout India; it is enacted as follows:

1. Repealed: (Repealed by the Repealing Act, 1870 (14 of 1870) Section 1 and Sch., Part II).

2. Articles of charge to be drawn out for public inquiry into conduct of certain public ser-vants: - Whenever the Government shall be of opinion that there are good grounds for making a formal and public inquiry into the truth of any imputation of misbehaviour by any person in the service of the Government, not removable from his appointment without the sanction of the Government it may cause the substance of the imputations to be drawn into distinct articles of charge, and may order a formal and public inquiry to be made into the truth thereof.

3. Authorities to whom inquiry may be committed. Notice to accused :-

The inquiry may be committed either to the Court, Board or other authority to which the person accused is subordinate, or to any other person or persons, to be specially appointed by the Govern-ment, Commissioners for the purpose; notice of which Commission shall be given to the person accused ten days at least before the beginning of the inquiry.

4. Conduct of Government prosecution:- When the Government shall think fit to conduct the prosecution, it shall nominate some person to conduct the same on its behalf.

5. Charge by accuser to be written and verified. Penalty for false accusation. Institution of inquiry by Government :- When the charge shall be brought by an accuser, the Government shall require the accusation to be reduced to writing, and verified by the oath or solemn affirmation of the accuser; and every person who shall wilfully and maliciously make any false accusation under this Act, upon such oath or affirmation, shall be liable to the penalties of perjury, but this enactment shall not be construed to prevent the Government from instituting any inquiry which it shall think fit without such accusation on oath or solemn affirmation as aforesaid.

6. Security from accuser left by Government to prosecute:- Where the imputations shall have been made by an accuser, and the Government shall think fit to leave to him the conduct of the prosecution, the Government before appointing the Commission shall require him to furnish reasonable security that he will attend and prosecute the charge thoroughly and effectually, and also will be forthcoming to answer any counter-charge or action which may be afterwards brought against him for malicious prosecution or perjury or subordinate of perjury, as the case may be.

7. Power of Government to abandon prosecution and to allow accuser to continue it :- At any subsequent stage of the proceedings, the Government may, if it think fit abandon the prosecution, and in such case may, if it think fit, on the application of the accuser, allow him to continue the prosecution, if he is desirous of so doing, on his furnishing such security as is hereinbefore mentioned.

8. Powers of Commissioners. Their protection. Service of their process. Powers of Court, etc., acting under Commission:- The Commissioners shall have the same power of punishing contempts and obstructions to their proceedings as is given to Civil and Criminal Courts by the Code of Criminal Procedure, 1898, and shall have the same powers for the summons of witnesses, and for compelling the production of documents, and for the discharge of their duty under the Commission, and shall be entitled to the same protection as the Zilla and City Judges, except that all process to cause the attendance of witnesses or other compulsory process, shall be served through and executed by the Zilla or City Judge in whose jurisdiction the witness or other person resides, on whom the process is to be served, and if he resides within Calcutta, Madras or Bombay, then through the Supreme Court of Judicature thereto. When the Commission has been issued to a Court, or other person or persons having power to issue such process in the exercise of their ordinary authority, they may also use all such power for the purposes of the Commission.

9. Penalty for disobedience to process:- All persons disobeying any lawful process issued as aforesaid for the purposes of the Commission shall be liable to the same penalties as if the same had issued originally from the Court or other authority through whom it is executed.

10. Copy of charge and list to be furnished to accused :- A Copy of the articles of charge,and list of the documents and witnesses by which each charge is to be sustained, shall be delivered to the person accused, at least three days before the beginning of the inquiry, exclusive of the day of delivery and the first day of the inquiry.

11. Procedure at beginning of inquiry. Non-appearance of accused and admission of charge:- At the beginning of the inquiry the prosecutor shall exhibit the articles of charge to the Commissioners, which shall be openly read, and the person accused shall thereupon be required to plead 'guilty' or 'not guilty' to each of them, which pleas shall be forthwith recorded with the articles of charge. If the person accused refuses, or without reasonable cause neglects, to appear to answer the charge either personally or by his counsel or agent, he shall be taken to admit the truth of the articles of charge.

12. Prosecutor's right of address:- The prosecutor shall then be entitled to address the Commissioners in explanation of the articles of charge, and of the evidence by they are to be proved; his address shall not be recorded.

13. Evidence for prosecution and examination of witnesses. Re-examination by prosecutor:- The oral and documentary evidence for the prosecution shall then be exhibited; the witnesses shall be examined by or on behalf of the prosecutor and may be cross-examined by or on behalf of the person accused. The prosecutor shall be entitled to reexamine the witnesses on any points on which they have been cross-examined, but not on any new matter, without leave of the Commissioners, who also may put such questions as they think fit.

14. Power to admit or call for new evidence for prosecution. Accused's right to adjournment:- If it shall appear necessary before the close of the case for the prosecution, the Commissioners may, in their discretion allow the prosecutor to exhibit evidence not included in the list given to the person accused, or may themselves call for new evidence; and in such case the person accused shall be entitled to have, if he demand it, an adjournment of the proceedings for three clear days, before the exhibition of such new evidence exclusive of the day of adjournment and of the day to which the proceedings are adjourned.

15. Defence of accused. To be recorded only when written:- When the case for the prosecution is closed, the person accused shall be required to make his defence, orally or in writing, as he shall prefer. If made orally, it shall not be recorded; if made in writing; it shall be recorded, after being openly read, and in that case a copy shall be given at the same time to the prosecutor.

16. Evidence for defence and examination of witnesses:- The evidence for the defence shall then be exhibited, and the witnesses examined, who shall be liable to cross-examination and re-examination to the examination by the Commissioners according to the like rules as the witnesses for the prosecution.

17. Examination of witnesses and evidence by prosecutor:- [Repealed by the Repealing Act, 1876 (12 of 1876), Section 1 and Schedule, Part I].

18. Notes of oral evidence:- The Commissioners or some person appointed by them shall take notes in English of all oral evidence, which shall be read aloud to each witness by whom the same was given, and, if necessary, explained to him in the language in which it was given, and shall be recorded with the proceedings.

19. Inquiry when closed with defence. Prosecutor when entitled to reply and give evidence. Accused not entitled to adjournment :- If the person accused makes only an oral defence, and exhibits no evidence, the inquiry shall end with his defence; if he records a written defence, or exhibits evidence the prosecutor shall be entitled to a general oral reply on the whole case, and may also exhibit evidence to contradict any evidence exhibited for the defence, in which case the person accused shall not be entitled to any adjournment of the proceedings, although such new evidence were not included in the list furnished to him.

20. Power to require amendment of charge and to adjourn. Reasons for refusing adjournment to be recorded:- When the Commissioners shall be of opinion that the articles of charge or any of them are not drawn with sufficient clearness and precision. The Commissioners may, in their discretion, require the same to be amended, and may thereupon, on the application of the person accused, adjourn the inquiry for a reason able time. The Commissioners may also, if they think fit adjourn the inquiry from time to time, on the application of either the prosecutor or the person accused on the ground of sickness or unavoidable absence of any witness or other reasonable cause. When such application is made and refused, the Commissioners shall record the application, and their reasons for refusing to comply with it.

21. Report of Commissioners' proceedings:- After the close of the inquiry the Commissioners shall forthwith report to Government to their proceedings under the Commission, and shall send with the record thereof their opinion upon each of the articles of charge separately, with such observations as they think fit on the whole case.

22. Power to call for further evidence or explanation- Inquiry into additional articles of charge. Reference of report of Special Commissioners' final orders: - The Government, on consideration of the report of the Commissioners, may order them to take further evidence, or give further explanation of their opinions. It may also order additional articles of charge to be framed, in which case the inquiry into the truth of such additional articles shall be made in the same manner as is herein directed with respect to the original charges. When Special Commissioners have been appointed, the Government may also, if it thinks fit, refer the report of the Commissioners to the Court or other authority to which the person accused is subordinate, for their opinion on the case, and will finally pass such orders thereon as appear just and consistent with its powers in such cases.

23. Definition of Government:- In this Act, " the Government" means the Central Government in the case of persons employed under that Government and the State Government in the case of persons employed under that Government. [G.S.R.199.dt.7.2.1967,Gaz.of Ind.,18-2-1967, Pt. II Sec.(i) P.229]

24. Saving of enactments as to dismissal of certain officers- Commission under Act for their trial:- Nothing in this Act shall be construed to repeal any Act or Regulation in force for the suspension or dismissal of Principal and other Sadar Amins or of Deputy Magistrates or Deputy Collectors, but a Commission may be issued for the trial of any charge against any of the said officers, under this Act, in any case in which the Government shall think it expedient.

25. Saving of power of removal without inquiry under Act:- Nothing in this Act shall be construed to affect the authority of Government, for suspending or removing any public servant for any cause without an inquiry under this Act.

SUBJECT INDEX

LIST OF CASE CITATIONS

Western India Match Company v. Paratha Sarathi (1956) I LLJ 151;Page 2

Bhikam Bobla v. Punjab State AIR 1963 Punj 255;Page 2

Chulsa Tea Co. v. Workmen Cal Gaz.,Part I-C,dt. 31.07.1969, p.285 (IT); Page 7

Trustees of Port of Bombay v. Bombay Port Trust Employees' Union 1956 ICR 552 (LAT); Page 7

Mukhtar Singh v. State of U.P. AIR 1957 All 297, 301; Page 7

G. Nageswar Rao v. A.P.S.R.T. Corporation, AIR 1959 SC 308; Page 10

Mukhtar Singh v. State AIR 1957 All HC 297 (30); Page 10

A.K. Kraipak V. Union of India (AIR 1970 SC 150); Page 10

Ramjibhai Ukabhai Parmer v. Manilal Purushottam Solanki AIR 1960 Guj 19; Page 10

Sunil Kumar Ghose v. Ajit Kumar, AIR 1969 Cal 492; Page 13

Mukhtar Singh v. State, AIR 1957 All 297 (30); Page 13

C. P. Govil v. Union of India 1965 DLT 16 (DB); Page 15

Anjali v. SBI 1993 (2) Bank CLR 372; Page 15, 16

Som Dutt V. Union Of India (AIR 1969 SC 414); Page 16

Nagar Palika, Nataur v. U.P. Public Services Tribunal, Lucknow, 1998 SCC (L&S)567; Page 17

Chulsa Tea Co. v. Workmen, Cal Gaz., Part I-C, dt. 31.07.1969, p.285; Page 18

Trustees of Port of Bombay v. Bombay Port Trust Employees' Union 1956 ICR 552 (LAT); Page 18

Tata Oil Mills Co. Ltd. v. Workmen, AIR 1965 SC 155; Page 23

Hindustan Petroleum Corporation v. H. L. Trehan, (1989) I SCC 764; Page 24

A.R.S.Choudhary v. Union of India, AIR 1956 Cal 662; Page 24

Kapur Singh v. Union of India, AIR 1956 Punj. 58; Page 25

Laxmi Devi Sugar Mills v. Nand Kishore (1956) II LLJ 439:AIR 1957 SC 7; Page 26

Paru Silk Mills Vikhroli v. Shamsuddin Abdulhuq, 1954 ICR 1047 (IC Bom.); Page 26

Sur Enamel and Stamping Works Ltd. V. Workmen, 1993 II LLJ 367(SC); Page 26

Krishna Chandra Tandon v. Union Of India (1974) 4 SCC 374; Page 27

Powari Tea Estate v. M.K.Barktaki (1965 II LLJ 102); Page 27

Management of Jagjit Beverages v. Workmen, Delhi Govt. Gazette, Dt. 11.06.59, Part VI, P 250 (IT); Page 27

Tata Chemicals Limited v. Workmen, AIR 1964, Guj. 265; Page 40

Narayan Amar v. Rajkumar Mills Ltd., 1960 I LLJ 654 (IT); Page 41

Indian Iron and Steel Co. Ltd., v. Workmen Cal. Gaz., Part I C, dt. 26.12.1968 p. 1445 (IT); Page 42

M.M. Siddiqui v. Union of India, AIR 1965, All 568; Page 42

Ishwar Narain v. Union Of India, AIR 1957, All 439; Page 42

T.C. Nilamegham Pillai v. Secretary of State, AIR, 1937 Mad.; Page 42

K. S. Rao v. State of A.P. AIR 1957 A.P. 414;Page 43

Punjab National Bank v. Punjab National Bank Employees' Federation, AIR, 1960, SC, 160, 173; Page 43

High Court of Calcutta v. Amal Kumar Roy, AIR 1962 SC 1704; Page 45

National Engineering Employees Union V.R.N. Kulkarni, (1968) II LLJ 82 Bombay (DB); Page 46

Workmen of Firestone Tyre and Rubber Co. of India Ltd vs Management 1975,I LLJ 278 (SC); Page 48

Motipur Sugar Factory Case, (1965) 2 LLJ 162 27 FJR 376: AIR 1965 SC 1803; Page 48

Chakravorty v. Union of India AIR 1956 Cal 662; Page 49

Abdul Wajeed v. State of Karnataka, 1981(1) SLR 454 (Kar.); Page 49

C. Nagaraja Bhat v. Canara Bank, 1987(3) Kar. L.J. 232; Page 50

State of Mysore v. Shivabasappa Shivappa, (1964 ILLJ SC, per Venkatrama Ayyar); Page 51

State of Haryana v. Rattan Singh (1982 ILLJ 46 SC); Page 51

Central Bank of India Ltd. V. Prakash Chand Jain (1969) II LLJ 377 SC; Page 52

Laxmi Devi Sugar Mills v. Ram Swaroop, (1957) I LLJ 17: AIR 1957 SC 82; Page 53

Brook Bond Company of India Ltd. v. Subba Raman, (1961) II LLJ 417: 20 FJR 424 (SC); Page 53

Shyamlal Gupta v. Workmen Cal. Gaz., Part I C, dt. 17.03.1966 p.195; Page 56

Ramnaresh Kumar v. State of West Bengal, (1958 ILLJ 567, 571 CAL.DB.); Page 64

Balvantary Ratilal Patil v. State of Maharashtra, (1968) II LLJ 700, 703 (SC); Page 64

Nepal Chandra Guchit v. District Magistrate, (1966, IILLJ 71 Calcutta); Page 64

Hemant Kumar Bhattacharya v. S.N. Mukherjee, AIR 1954, Calcutta 340 (DB); Page 64

Sankar Pillai v. Kerala State, (1950 ILLJ 621 Ker.); Page 65

Madhavan v. Commissioner of Income Tax (1983 IILLJ 356 Ker); Page 65

Rashiklal Nandlal V. Bank of Baroda (1956 ILLJ 103 Lat.); Page 65

Bharat Bank Ltd. V. Employees reported in AIR 1950 SC 188; Page 66

Hajee Ismail Said & Sons (P) Ltd. v. Fourth Industrial Tribunal, AIR 1966 Cal 375: (1966) II LLJ 59; Page 66

Case Citations

Anand Narain Shukla v. State of M.P., (1980) I SCC 252; Page 148

Benares Electric Light & Power Co. Ltd. v. Hanuman Singh,(1972) 2 LLJ 19 (SC); Page 151

Rohtak and Hissar Distt. Electric Supply Co. v. State, AIR 1966 SC 1471; Page 151

www.ingramcontent.com/pod-product-compliance
Lightning Source LLC
Chambersburg PA
CBHW021925190326
41519CB00009B/911